T0289464

Isabel Verstraete

# DOES YOUR BRAND CARE?

building a better world with
the C A R E Principles

Lannoo
Campus

D/2021/45/74 – ISBN 978 94 014 7503 7 – NUR 802, 800

Cover design and illustrations: Lucia Biancalana
Interior design: Wendy De Haes

LannooCampus Publishers is a subsidiary of Lannoo Publishers,
the book and multimedia division of Lannoo Publishers nv.

LannooCampus Publishers
Vaartkom 41 box 01.02      P.O. Box 23202
3000 Leuven               1100 DS Amsterdam
Belgium                   Netherlands
www.lannoocampus.com

# Contents

**CHAPTER 1**
Why I developed the C A R E Principles: a personal note       6

**CHAPTER 2**
The 'next normal': tooling up for constant change       12

**CHAPTER 3**
Why brands should start showing they care today –
if they want to thrive tomorrow       18

**CHAPTER 4**
The C A R E Principles: how collaboration, agility, reliability
and empathy can make your brand future-proof       26

**CHAPTER 5**
Why Collaboration is key       36

**CHAPTER 6**
Why Agility matters       52

**CHAPTER 7**
Why Reliability is crucial       80

**CHAPTER 8**
Why Empathy works       100

**CHAPTER 9**
Embracing the new kids on the block: Generations Z and Alpha       124

**CHAPTER 10**
The C A R E SCAN: How much does your company C A R E?       134

**THANKS!**       138

**ABOUT**       140

**PRAISE FOR *DOES YOUR BRAND CARE?***       142

**END NOTES**       148

# CHAPTER 1

# Why I developed the C A R E Principles: a personal note

I must have been about five years old when I was on holiday in Spain with my mother and grandparents. We spent the last afternoon on a sunny Spanish beach. Shops filled with colourful plastic beach toys caught my attention. I asked my mum if I could go and check them out. She agreed but told me not to cross the street.

I was in total awe of the sheer quantity of beach balls, shovels, buckets, pails and inflatables in every shape and colour. I wandered off with my head in the clouds, filled with the rainbow vision I had just seen. Without knowing that this would become part of my job, I was researching variations in products between one shop and another. Every next shop seemed to have something slightly different and even more appealing to my little self. I revelled in the vibrant colours of all these plastic toys, compared the holiday drawings on the beach balls, was mesmerized by the shapes of inflatable boats and colourful air mattresses, and lost all track of time and place.

I was completely captured by the intense, powerful message communicated by this beach gear: 'Buy me and you'll have fun on the beach!' Suddenly I found myself crying, surrounded by people talking to me in a language I didn't understand. Not much later, my mum picked me up from a local police station. That last night in the hotel, my mum tried to dance but that proved difficult with me literally stuck to her legs, afraid of losing her. A feeling I never wanted to experience again: my mum was my anchor in life.

This anecdote summarizes my life quite well. I have always been curious, always interested in what was around the next corner or under the surface of things, fascinated by products, brands and retail. Today, I am still walking with my head in the clouds, searching for something to spot, something to discover, something new to surprise me. Today, I still can't pass a beachfront toy store without feeling the energy and sparkle these shops have always given me!

My mother—who has always been a tremendous example in my life—always trusted me and stimulated my curiosity and desire to get the most out of life. My fulfilling life has given me two daughters, Lua and Rocky, and a loving boyfriend, Rob, with whom I have spent more than a decade of my life. Career stops took me to Paris, Brussels and Amsterdam, and now I live and work in Antwerp.

I have worked on the corporate side of the fence and for advertising agencies. My biggest motivation in my work has always been the ability to help brands. In 2011, I realized more than ever that I couldn't help brands any longer from within an advertising agency. The role and effect of advertising was about to change due to digitization.

I launched my own brand strategy consultancy and a couple of years later Kate Stockman crossed my path on an international repositioning campaign. The assignment ended up in the formation of Stockmanverstraete. Together we had a successful business venture, leading strategic assignments in marketing, branding, strategy, communication and innovation.

Near the end of 2019, I was about to start a major repositioning assignment for a well-known corporate brand. My agenda was filled to bursting for the next couple of months when I received the news that my mother had terminal skin cancer. After a sleepless night and a phone call to my business partner, I withdrew from the job and started to take care of my mother full-time. My life took a serious turn, as I mainly spent time with my mother when the Covid-19 lockdown came. More painful news soon followed when my father was also diagnosed with cancer. While my father was recovering from his operation and treatment, my mum died on a sunny day in July. Hoping to have finished this book before she passed away, I knew I had lost the race. This devastating experience, coming at the same time as a deadly virus racing through the world, gave me grief, sorrow and stress. I wanted to go back to a world free of this deadly new disease. A world in which I could continue my beloved job. A world in which my parents were healthy, and I could hold them tight. A world in which my adolescent daughters could live the life of youngsters as we had known it.

> **It's only when the tide goes out that you learn who has been swimming naked.**
>
> **Warren Buffett, investor**

However, I realized pretty soon that the world as we knew it wouldn't return, and that the turbulence we are facing today has been building up since long before the current health crisis. I saw that the world had flipped and that business as usual wouldn't return. I wondered: Am I doing the right thing? Isn't it time for me—a brand consultant who always sells her advice—to flip my business as well and start to focus on doing the right thing? My biggest motivation in my work has always been the ability to help brands: Am I helping them in the best way now? I asked myself these questions over and over again …

So I paused, took a few steps back and felt a sudden urge to study, to research, to listen, to learn and to understand the world in which we had landed. I looked at my own profession and the world with fresh eyes. Realizing that if we want to evolve to a place of greater fairness and safety for our planet and its people, I came to the conclusion that we genuinely need to rethink the way we live and what we do.

We need to face our attitudes, our priorities and our compassion.
We need to reconsider what and how we consume.
We need to think about what we stand for and how we voice that.
We live in a polarized society in which the negative voices, controversial sentiments and oppositions are growing. In this society, it is important to highlight what goes well, and it is time to resist negative voices in society, to counter them with positive action.
And we need to act now, for ourselves and our children, and not leave the burden of the mess we're in on their shoulders.

I am rebelling against inertia, negativity, apathy and cynicism. In the early days of the first lockdown, I launched a daily post on all my social media: 'Positive News of the Day'. I did this because I strongly believe that there are good reasons to be hopeful and positive about the future. I believe that there is a very real current of change and that we can all—individual by individual—help to make the world a better place. We need to realize that we can all change, that we can use our voices as a positive force. These 'Positive News of the Day' posts gave me some oxygen in the midst of the pandemic. It was great to see so many amazing examples of companies that care for more than just earning money. It felt good to pass on this oxygen to others and to focus on what matters, not on what sells.

So I continued to search every day for positive signals of change. This little project of mine was the beginning of a completely new chapter of my life. In my daily research, I saw so many brands that managed to adapt—seemingly without effort—to numerous and rapid changes in society. I analyzed the companies that seemed to deal better with the crisis, and I discovered a pattern driving their success.

This pattern is marked by a shift in attitude towards the way they do business. These brands dare to showcase a softer, more caring version of themselves. These companies have understood that in order to remain in business, they now need to focus more on solving than on selling. Out of the 'Positive News of the Day' posts grew a vision for a book, a web platform for positive change and the C A R E Scan, a new methodology for helping brands prepare for this new normal in which we have landed. Sharing my ideas and providing positive inspiration was definitely the thing that kept me going in these challenging times.

So, I wrote down the knowledge I had built up over the thirty years of my career. I combined it with newfound wisdom gleaned from online lessons, gathering insights from authors much smarter than me, such as Simon Sinek, and conversations with highly respected friends, clients and business contacts who generously granted me their time. I connected the dots between what I experienced in my job as a consultant and what I see ahead of us. Enjoy the book: I can only hope it sparkles with the positive changes the world needs, bright and shiny like so many colourful beach toys on a sunny day.

I guess it's clear that I'm a born optimist—you might even call me a 'new optimist'—as I believe we need to focus on what matters, not on what sells. I'm also a doer, so in addition to this book, you'll find even more positive inspiration from brands that care on my web platform and in my video podcasts. You can take classes on how to inject CARE into your company or you can take a C A R E Scan and find out how well your brand scores on the C A R E Principles.

Take care,
Isabel

PS: I dedicate this book to my mother, who taught me to fearlessly believe in myself, and to my daughters, who challenge me every day to become a more caring version of myself. This one is for you, my girls!

# CHAPTER 2

# The 'next normal': tooling up for constant change

It goes without saying that companies already do a lot of good things and entrepreneurs are working hard to keep their companies thriving. Everybody today is working on sustainability goals. CEOs understand that they need to be flexible in order to keep millennials on board. In terms of holiday entitlements, European countries have the best scores; Belgian employees even have an average of thirty-four holidays a year![1]

Thanks to the pandemic, nearly all employers have finally introduced digital and flexible working. Most employees will keep it once the health situation has stabilized. Homeworking is here to stay. While many companies are already doing their best, some are starting to feel as if doing their best isn't quite enough.

What will business look like tomorrow? Well, it will look quite different to what it does now, which is why you'll need to think now and act tomorrow if you want to adapt your company to the next normal,[2] because we have indeed landed in a turbulent decade. In the old days, business life was pretty simple and straightforward. You were running a business and making money, and most of your employees worked for you for their entire career. Companies were black boxes to anyone who didn't work there. Back then, customers hardly had a voice, let alone thought of using it. They were just buying products and services based on their personal taste and how much they were prepared to spend.

Marketing made a difference by building brand awareness and by developing brand preference. In pretty much any sector, you had an 'A' brand which was considered 'the best and most expensive' option on the market, followed by some cheaper and less performant brands. Life was simple and clear. In the first decade of this century, attributes beyond the mere commercial entered the picture. Brands had to explain to consumers where they were sourcing, whether their manufacturing process was environmentally friendly and how they treated their own employees. Still, that didn't seem too complicated either.

Fast forward to today. People are openly questioning companies on their behaviour. Critical journalism platforms, some newspapers and consumer organizations are fuelling these feelings of distrust and are openly questioning the morality of brands. Brand boycotts and the naming and shaming of companies have become powerful tools for exposing companies that think they can continue with 'business as usual' while pretending they care.

Companies are facing a new reality in which some of their customers have bigger and stronger social media platforms than they do. These consumer voices sometimes become more powerful than the brand's own voice, and are often considered more honest, authentic and true. Businesses no longer compete in the commercial arena but in the ethical and moral arena, and this is not a fleeting phenomenon: this is what people will expect from now on. Companies will have to examine thorny issues and either alleviate or resolve them. Both people and the planet we live on are on the brink of catastrophe—something we'll dive further into later on. Businesses must find a new balance between commercial and moral objectives.

The C A R E Principles start from a core belief that spreads out in three simple mantras:

1. **It is about the future**
   (and nobody really cares how good your brand was in the past).

2. **It is about your clients**
   (and not about enriching yourself).

3. **It is about their lives**
   (and not about your challenges).

Change in society today occurs at a much faster pace than changes within company walls—that's a fact. The gap between where the world is heading and what companies can do about it is widening. In order to close this gap, and in order to achieve success, organizations must undergo a transformation: from being strictly business enterprises to being social enterprises as well. Companies tomorrow will be valued as much for their interaction with and impact on society as for their financial results.

Some organizations—such as B Certified Corporation,[3] for example—deserve special mention. It is an amazing initiative that was launched by three friends who left careers in business and private equity to create an organization dedicated to making it easier for mission-driven companies to protect and improve their positive impact over time. Certified B Corporations are companies that balance profit and purpose. The certification requires them to legally consider the impact of their decisions on their workers, customers, suppliers, community and environment. These certified businesses are proving that competing to be not only 'best in the world' but also 'best for the world' is a winning strategy!

> ## You can't be a part of a solution if you don't recognize how you are a part of the problem.
>
> **Elaine Welteroth, American journalist**

So, sure, your corporate social responsibility plan and your marketing purpose were a very good start and will differentiate you from your competitors today. That is fine for now. However, it is not enough for tomorrow. In order to remain ahead of your competitors, you will need to make a profound shift in your manner of thinking and doing, and in the way you approach business. The C A R E Principles will help you make this shift at your own pace, with the right, unique mix that fits your company's true nature and feels honest and authentic.

It's good not
only to be best
in the world,
but also best
for the world.

# CHAPTER 3

# Why brands should start showing they care today–if they want to thrive tomorrow

Today the world is in the midst of a health crisis, a social crisis, an economic crisis, an environmental crisis and a psychological crisis all rolled into one. Covid-19 caused them to snowball. This harsh reality causes a lot of grief. To deal with grief, frustration and setbacks, people used to turn to religious or political leaders in search of help. Today, in many countries, belief in religion has faded. Political leaders in many democracies find themselves in a weakened position, and political systems divided along the ideological lines of 'left' and 'right' feel archaic and out of date. Some political leaders cling to power using techniques as old as the Roman Empire: techniques including violence, excessive control and propaganda in the form of fake news.

People are beginning to realize that many things have been going wrong, and it feels as if the whole world is racing at a speed that no longer seems under control. Civilian protests, demonstrations and commotion on a small or large scale is revealing the gap between those in command and the average Joe. People have lost trust. They are suspicious of those in power, a feeling that was present long before Covid-19! This loss of trust in the once powerful institutions that kept the world running is visible in all kinds of research worldwide. **Edelman** Intelligence,[4] a global insight and analytics consultancy, conduct a yearly global survey on trust. Their Trust Barometer[5] demonstrates how people have lost trust in governments, media and companies over the last few years. In 2019[6] however, an overwhelming number of people—a whopping 81%—were looking at brands and asking them to do the right thing!

2019 Edelman Trust Barometer Special Report:
In Brands We Trust?

**A NEED FOR BRANDS
TO DO THE RIGHT THING**

Percent who say this is a deal breaker or deciding factor
in their brand buying decision

I must be able to **trust the brand** to
do what is right

⊥

**81**%

This creates a huge opportunity for companies to step in and do just that. But with great opportunity comes great responsibility. Your company will have to make a fundamental decision: stay the same and remain part of the problem or adapt and work towards a solution. Several companies have already understood the need to shift gears, ethically speaking, and are changing course by becoming more engaged. They have found charities to which they can donate and their marketing departments have developed a higher purpose. Their mission statements express how much they value their staff and their clients.

Without doubt, these are all great ways to stimulate goodwill among certain stakeholders and consumers. It is definitely a step in the right direction. But in order to really make a positive change, companies need to ask themselves how they can play a role in people's lives. How can they show they care about their staff, their clients, their communities? How can they understand their fears and dreams? How can they help allay the first and achieve the second? Understanding that it is not about words but about actions is one of the biggest shifts brands are facing today. Because, let's face it, people can only be happy about your sustainability efforts or your rainforest alliances if they have the basics of their own lives straightened out, and if they feel that your efforts for the planet overlap with their own concerns. Tomorrow it won't be enough to have your company values on the wall while underpaying your workers.[7] It won't be acceptable to support the World Wide Fund for Nature (WWF)[8] while destroying the rainforest in search of resources.

Obviously, some companies will continue to try to cut corners at the expense of their staff, their community, their country and the planet. Most companies won't act on positive change because they suddenly became philanthropists. No, they will do it under the pressure of several generations. Fuelled by young people who don't understand why they have to pay the price for the disasters left to them by the previous generations. These young consumers will become even more demanding on issues such as ethical behaviour and transparency. Working for a company that doesn't walk the talk will become an obstacle for many employees, and thus the cost of hiring talent will continue to rise.

Companies will need to express themselves loud and clear about what they stand for and how they will show that they care. Not through mission statements, freshly painted values or advertising campaigns, but through an open, honest and authentic relationship with their employees, clients and communities. Companies will need to prove that they can be trusted on every level, that they really do mean well.

The overall insight behind the C A R E Principles is about—well, caring: taking care of someone or something. Anyone can care. Taking care is not about how deep your pockets are, but about how big your heart is. Success definitely lies ahead for companies that realize they need to be outspoken about the things they care about. Brands can become powerful forces for positive change in society and they are in a position to lead the way by taking responsibility. So you should ask yourself: What side do you want your company to be on? Do you want to remain part of the problem, or will you be part of the solution?

Frankly, there are no real guidelines when it comes to caring—there are so many ways to care, and so many things to care about! The important lesson about care is that it needs to be authentic: it needs to resonate with your true nature. Care comes from the heart. It is not a marketing tool for changing your brand image. Care is a way of facing outwards: of engaging with the world on myriad levels, whether by reaching out to those closest to you or launching a platform to help save the world. Reaching out, lending a helping hand, marshalling others for a good cause—these are all effective ways of caring. In the following three examples, I share stories of brands that show they care in ways that are natural and authentic to their DNA, from simple gestures to a concerted campaign.

Sometimes even a kind gesture in difficult times is enough to show you care. Loom,[9] an American video platform, lowered their prices and made their service free of charge for all American students and teachers as soon as the pandemic hit the world.[10]

Taking care doesn't have to disrupt your business model, either. It can be very small and very local. Take the example of Jumbo, a Dutch supermarket. At more than forty of their stores, they have installed a 'kletskassa'—a novelty that can be roughly translated as 'chat register'[11]—at which elderly people or anyone who's feeling lonely can have a little chat with the lady behind the counter. Although they launched this caring idea before the pandemic, it is a great way of getting a feel for the worries of your clients. So many people are lonely and have no one to talk to. Jumbo understood this and acted upon it.

Of course, care can also be big and ambitious and world saving, as in the case of the American brand Patagonia.[12] This socially aware, eco-conscious brand was inspired by young American climate activists, so in 2019 they launched their 'Facing extinction' campaign.[13] They not only urged people to join the climate strikes, but also closed their offices and stores to allow their own staff to march for

> **Obtaining financial results is a consequence, not a goal.**
>
> **Miguel Patricio, CEO Kraft Heinz**

a better climate. As an activist brand of the first hour—this is their true nature, as Patagonia has always been at the forefront of sustainability and social matters—they were well positioned to call others to action, asking people to tell Congress that there is no room in government for climate deniers. A great campaign and a beautiful and authentic way to show care!

However you want to show you care, the choices are endless—it's entirely up to you! In the next chapter, we'll dive right into the C A R E Principles model. It is simple, straightforward and structured. You'll be taking C A R E of your people, your clients, your communities and the world in no time at all!

Care will help companies face **new roles and responsibilities that will be more about solving than selling**. If your clients believe in your motives, financial success will follow. Obtaining financial results will become a consequence, not a goal. In the next chapters, we'll examine the four other attitude shifts contained in the C A R E Principles. In the process, I'll showcase brands that got ahead of the competition by applying them. Even though it might seem like a huge upheaval at first, injecting the C A R E Principles into your company can be accomplished step by step. We're not talking about a revolution, but about a necessary *evolution* your company needs to make in order to remain relevant in the future. In the old days, marketing and advertising shaped your brand; tomorrow, your brand will be shaped by who you really are. And that will become your primary differentiator.

The C A R E Principles can help your brand stand out from the crowd. Transforming your brand into a brand that shows it cares and therefore matters is not that difficult. Successful cases prove that injecting CARE into your company is not about investing more, it is about investing differently. It's not rocket science, folks, it's pretty simple: all you need to do is become aware of your brand's new roles and responsibilities and consciously take them into consideration.

This book highlights brands that show they have already understood the importance of care. Not focusing on companies that abuse their power is a deliberate choice. Seeking out those brands—big and small, known and unknown, from all over the world—that make a difference and naming them is also a deliberate choice. Call it naming and 'faming', rather than naming and shaming. Take inspiration from the example of these trailblazers and how they were able to start positive change today. You can, too: step by step, day by day, action by action.

Finally, I use the words brand, company, organization, business, and enterprise interchangeably throughout the book, because it no longer matters in what industry you work, who your target group is and whether or not you advertise. Everybody is a brand: small, large, start-up, business-to-business or business-to-consumer. Forget the old divisions and focus on how your target group sees you: as a brand!

**With great opportunity comes great responsibility.**

# CHAPTER 4

# The C A R E Principles: how collaboration, agility, reliability and empathy can make your brand future-proof

COLLABORATION

AGILITY

RELIABILITY

EMPATHY

Showing you care is a great start and might already differentiate you from others. However, developing the C A R E Principles on a deeper level can help you take a leap into the future. Applying the four principles of **collaboration**, **agility**, **reliability** and **empathy** needs to be carried out in the right proportions, the unique mix that fits best with your company's DNA.

It is not a one-size-fits-all solution.

It is not a quick fix.

COLLABORATION          AGILITY          RELIABILITY          EMPATHY

The ability to adapt your company's behaviour in becoming a more collaborative, agile, reliable and empathic version of yourself will take time.

Applying these Principles entails a profound adaptation of your organization, your structure, your processes and your way of thinking.

It is important to understand why these four Principles matter and why they need to be accelerated.

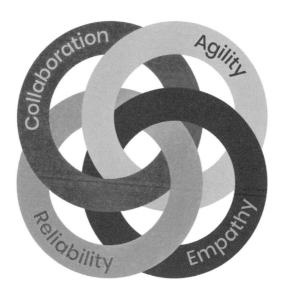

The good news is:
- you can do this step by step,
- some transformations can be accomplished without extra costs,
- most can be applied by start-ups, SMEs and multinationals alike,
- they can be introduced on a small scale without interrupting your existing processes and platforms,
- it is not about more investment, but about shifting your investments,
- it is about a shift in attitude in the way you do business.

As the C A R E Principles are people-centred, it really starts first and foremost within your organization, with **your own people**. Note: I really dislike the term 'human resources', which seems to have been developed in an era when the human part didn't really matter and employees were considered just another resource to be exploited, like financial or natural resources ... Please keep in mind that they are more than just another 'resource' for making your business successful! Getting your people to work together as the best possible version of themselves and with contemporary tools and processes will make you a reliable and trustworthy employer. Understanding and acting on their needs, helping them surmount obstacles and clear hurdles, both within the company and in their private lives, will make you a more empathic company. Your people are really at the core of this model!

**YOUR PEOPLE**

Just as everything in our globalized world is interconnected, so it is with your business. You can have the best staff ever and be the most award-winning employer of modern times, but if you do not have—or do not have enough—clients, you won't last. So, the second level of the model deals with your reason for being: **your clients**! This level is all about creating a long-lasting relationship with them by understanding and anticipating their needs and desires. This is the part in which we have a look at marketing and customer service and how this domain has evolved recently. Are you ready to develop a long-term relationship with your clients? You can, if they believe that you can create value for them on all levels.

**YOUR CLIENTS**

While the two preceding levels might already have received a lot of your attention in the past, the next two levels may have remained in the dark by comparison. Taking care of **your communities** in the broad sense of the word is the next level of the C A R E model. This is not about classic shareholder value creation. This is about becoming a better version of yourself towards your suppliers, your local government, your neighbours—in short, towards all external stakeholders. Because, let's face it, your company is part of a community whether you like it or not. Eternal economic growth to make your shareholders wealthier can no longer be reconciled with the challenges facing the world. Becoming a stakeholder-oriented organization will, in the long run, also be good for the shareholders.

**YOUR COMMUNITY**

Finally, the last level is about the bigger picture in which we all live: **the world**. Driven by climate change and sustainability goals, this level is already on the agenda at most companies. Obviously, finding new and better ways of managing our resources is a massive part of our responsibility. But wait—I hear you asking— if it's so massive and important, why does it come last? One answer is that for many people, it's something far away, something intangible. Something so massive and so devastating that we see no beginning and no end, so most of us ignore it and continue to live as we have always lived. When parts of California or Australia burn down, or when the Artic sea is at its lowest level ever and scientists urge us to change our habits, or by 2050 catastrophes will start happening, most people really don't lose much sleep. Widespread ecological catastrophe is certainly difficult to grasp, and many people believe their individual behaviour won't matter if corporations and governments don't start trying harder to turn the tide. In the midst of the pandemic, for example, parts of the population and even some leaders continued to indulge in risky behaviour, as if there were no coronavirus. If your company can invest and focus on this level, by all means do so if it naturally fits with your company's DNA. If not, take care of the other levels first to build relevance towards your people, your clients and your communities.

**THE WORLD**

You can start changing the world one step at a time, and this model helps you tackle the issues ahead in a more structured way. Start at the heart of the matter: your own people! Even this first step brings you closer to change on other levels as well. Finally, introducing the C A R E Principles should start at the top. An entrepreneur or a CEO needs to lead by example and implement changes from above, showing his/her employees, clients, suppliers, vendors and other stakeholders that he/she really CAREs about this matter. It is definitely a top-down process if you want it to succeed.

The four levels of the C A R E model will be used throughout the book to structure the next four chapters, each devoted to one of the four C A R E Principles. Each level is amply illustrated with cases, successful brands to inspire you and show you how to inject C A R E into your company. At the end of each C A R E chapter is a list of free things you can do to embrace care at the heart of your organization. Zero cost, immediately implementable things to kickstart your road towards being a future-proof brand.

Let's dive into the mechanics of care and see why **collaboration** and partnership matter more than ever!

**This is not about classic shareholder value creation. This is about becoming a better version of yourself towards your suppliers, your local government, your neighbours – all external stakeholders!**

# CHAPTER 5

# Why Collaboration is key

Let's have a look at why collaboration and
partnerships will be key for a future-proof
company. You may already have realized that
dealing with the complex challenges we face
means that you'll need to reach out to others in
order to win the battle together. As strange as it
may seem, reaching out to others starts inside
your company, as you will need to break down
silos in order to outperform your competitors.
Why? Outperforming your competitors today is
one thing, but preparing your company to be
an attractive employer to the next generation
is another. Are you ready to empower small
teams, shift decision-making and speed up the
learning abilities of your staff? Let's see what
collaboration can be like from multiple angles.
We'll start by focusing on internal collaboration
within your own company. External collaboration
is explored in the client and community
sections. First, though, let's find out what
hurdles might be preventing your own people
from performing at a higher level.

## TODAY'S HURDLES

It may seem strange that companies need to start by working on their internal collaboration modes, as many will think they have no issues in that field. Well, think again. You might need to have a closer look at your internal organization and face reality. Several deep, compelling reasons often stand in the way of better internal collaboration. To name a few: in some companies, office workers feel superior to factory workers and refuse to collaborate in order to resolve issues that could help level up productivity. This attitude is frequently spotted at companies where the management has little respect for anybody below them. This kind of toxic internal culture might seem like a relic from the past, but unfortunately it is still around.

Another big hurdle to collaboration is connected to the fact that people spend an awful lot of time in meetings. Meetings in which no real decisions are taken. Meetings in which the bosses who are actually responsible for deciding are not present, so basically meetings that keep the people from their real job. For this reason, among others, collaboration with other departments is not encouraged at all in many organizations. There are often huge visible and invisible walls between departments. Department managers' main focus is to deliver maximum revenue and profit, often at the expense of other departments. That seems illogical, but it is the reality in most companies, as managers often get opposing KPIs.[14] Under such a regime, it's little wonder that the urge to collaborate is quite low, as people are punished financially for doing so.

Moreover, most companies are still hierarchically structured. This can make the organization slow and unprepared to adapt to the demands of the market. In this type of structure, younger employees in more junior positions often go unheard. With the technological issues facing most companies today, however, it might help to pull in these younger profiles in a more horizontal chain of command. In addition, transparency is often lacking due to internal bureaucracy. Having too many levels of management can obstruct internal communication and impede fast decision-making. Finally, in structures like this, power and responsibility are reserved for management levels throughout the organization, leaving little or no empowerment for the rest of the staff.

## TOMORROW'S IMPACT

With business's role in society being redefined and a new generation demanding a different approach to work, a deeper level of care is called for. And with automation, robotization and deep machine learning on our doorstep, we'll need to rethink workforce structure and working experience once and for all. This reinvention can be accomplished on different levels depending on your organization's readiness, size, goals, skills and market needs. But if you are convinced that your company should have a major rethink, be sure to include technology and to create something bold enough to meet societal changes. Lifelong learning, agile skills training, moving faster and adapting to a far more diverse workforce and world will definitely be part of your company's future challenges.

Let's see how you could stimulate collaboration on the four levels we introduced in the C A R E Principles:
- your people,
- your clients,
- your communities,
- the world.

## 1. YOUR PEOPLE

Strangely, the more technology driven the world becomes, the more it will come down to people making the difference. Technology is available to your competitors too. You'll be able to make a difference by focusing on the human side of things. Nourish the people you have and consider them from a different perspective to prepare them for the road ahead.

A hierarchical structure might still work out just fine for you. Amazon, with almost 900,000 employees worldwide, is a blockbuster and is built on a classic hierarchical structure. This organizational structure works for Amazon because the company is organized into a number of smaller teams under separate management. This structure allows managers to work more closely with their team members and facilitates control over their department. So, if it works for you, no need to fix it.

Still, if the world has flipped, it might be time to flip your company too. Showing an ability to respond more rapidly and accurately to the needs of your consumers, being prepared for digitization and new technologies, understanding the demographic changes and reacting to new competitors might prompt you to examine the benefits of a horizontal organizational structure. In order to become more versatile, department walls need to come down, literally. Horizontal networks, platform models or flat organizational structures can replace today's hierarchical structures. In a horizontal network, teams are formed temporarily for certain projects. Decisions are radically decentralized and made by the teams with regards to both the situation and project.

In a flat organizational structure, employees often have more responsibility and are more involved in important conversations. Transparency is also a big advantage when using a flat organizational structure thanks to the limited bureaucracy. Having fewer levels of management also simplifies internal communication and enables fast decision-making, and because the layers of middle management are removed, power and responsibility are divided more evenly throughout the organization. The dissolution of traditional structures encourages interdisciplinary collaboration between internal and external experts, too. This means that anybody can potentially be the 'boss' of a project, even a very junior person. In the next project, somebody else will take the lead. In this set-up, your staff is not pigeonholed according to age, experience or title. Depending on expertise, an employee can lead one project team and be led in another horizontal team. This "network thinking" stimulates internal communication and collaboration.

Choosing this type of structure also means embracing an experimental mood instead of a planning mood. Rethinking structures, roles and responsibilities can also bring new forms of leadership in which teamwork, rather than personal performance, is rewarded. Employees could be rewarded for cross-department projects, and personal bonuses could be reduced, as there is truth in the saying: 'talent wins games, but teamwork and intelligence win championships'. The ego-driven career and personal-performance focus in today's companies could shift towards collaborative performance.

Radical reorganization—though it can result in huge benefits—is something that needs to be done with care. It brings about a huge internal shift, and your employees might take years to adapt to a sudden, new model of responsibility and structure. Test change on a micro level first before rolling it out in the whole company. Stimulate internal collaboration on a project to start with and learn from the limitations the project encounters. Adjust and adapt the system until it works best for you and your people. There is no one-size-fits-all solution: every company must find its optimal form to perform. But embrace the idea of looking at your internal organization with fresh eyes, as it might need a reboot to withstand the turbulence ahead.

**CASE STUDY**

## How Covid-19 ramped up collaboration at a Brussels hospital

A great example of internal collaboration can be found today at **Brussels University Hospital**. Marc Noppen, CEO of this hospital, kept a diary during the lockdown for *De* *Tijd*, a Flemish newspaper. In a very honest weekly column, he explained to readers how hospitals had become large, slow, hierarchical organizations, and how even his own hospital suffered from this unfortunate trend. The sudden coronavirus outbreak shook them up and forced them to adopt a quick, flexible and agile management style that left the institution's nearly 4,000 employees plenty of responsibility and room for initiatives. He explained how before Covid-19, it would have taken dozens of meetings to decide on a new colour of wallpaper, while at the beginning of the first lockdown they did a complete overhaul of the organization and structure of the hospital in only three days. The virus taught him that:

• having a clear vision,
• clearly projecting goals and needs,
• showing clear leadership, and
• communicating all of the above in simple but clear guidelines

was enough to guide people as they took action themselves. It stimulated his staff to look for the right type of internal collaboration to make things happen. As there was no time to lose— the virus was upon us and hospitals needed to be ready to receive huge numbers of patients—a crash course in change management was executed.

About 700 employees started to work from home and had to reconfigure healthcare remotely. When asked the critical question as to whether his entire staff followed this sudden change in working methods, he replied that 10% didn't listen, didn't cope well or simply didn't do the work appropriately. But instead of focusing on this 10%, he preferred to stimulate the other 90%, who have proven to be open-minded about wanting to build the best possible hospital for their patients. Setting out clear goals, letting people see the bigger picture, leading by example and letting your staff figure out for themselves how they can achieve a change in plans is the spirit that Van Noppen applies now. He is a compelling voice in the public debate for more reforms of the public health system. Teleconsultations for general practitioners had been under debate for more than five years. During the corona crisis, it only took a handful of days to set it up successfully. Van Noppen can only hope that this, and other reforms aimed at modernizing hospitals and healthcare, will be introduced. He is definitely a game-changer and is currently advocating European-wide collaboration to tackle the next pandemic.

## 2. YOUR CLIENTS

Partnerships and collaborations are already a standard practice in the fashion, music and movie industry, often on a one-off basis: a temporary collaboration or a limited edition collection. Think of the designer collections that H&M bring to market each year. They started this successful initiative back in 2004 with Chanel designer Karl Lagerfeld. It was an instant hit, as it was the perfect strategy for marrying top designer brands with high street fashion. This collaboration model proved to be a win-win for both parties. However, joining forces with your clients is fairly uncommon, even though it is capable of generating great insights, building fan loyalty, creating a truly interactive relationship with your customer base and delivering interesting new products or services! Let's dive into the music industry, an industry that has been profoundly disrupted: first by Apple, now by the pandemic.

**CASE STUDY**

## Co-creating an album with fans

You have probably heard of the Northern Irish band **Snow Patrol**. Lead singer Gary Lightbody now lives in Los Angeles and was unable to get together with his bandmates when the pandemic hit the world. To entertain himself, and with no real plan in mind, he started weekly 'Saturday Songwrite' sessions on Instagram Live. It all started with him just singing songs and doing covers. Still without any real intentions, he started to ask people for chords and lyrics during an Instagram Live session. He wrote down as many lyrics as he could during the twenty-five-minute shout out. Then he went offline for an hour and pieced everything together into a song. 'Dance With Me'[15] was born, the first song to be created this way.

August 2020 saw the release of **The Fireside Sessions**,[16] an EP with five songs composed by Lightbody and his fans. The fans were credited as the 'Saturday Songwriters', while the other band members got involved in recording the songs. Everybody who participated in this unique project worked for free, and the revenue from the EP went to the Trussell Trust Charity, a network of foodbanks in the UK. Gary Lightbody said he has no clue when he will be back to touring and recording music like he did before, but he definitely enjoyed the process and may have launched an entirely new way of co-creating into the world!

## 3. YOUR COMMUNITIES

With so many challenges ahead of us—rapid globalization, fierce competition, social change, technological breakthroughs, scarcity of raw materials—businesses need to reinvent themselves continuously to cope. The future of collaboration in business needs to be seen through the prism of new and long-lasting partnerships. Expanded, creative, atypical partnerships. Partnerships that bring together a variety of stakeholders  and cover unexpected topics. When you think of your communities, you can tick many boxes: your neighbourhood, your local government, your suppliers, your vendors … the list of connections you have as a company is endless. Whatever you decide to do affects these connections.

There are many examples of collaboration, but in this chapter I would like to focus on those brave companies that dare to collaborate with their direct competitors. Two competing Belgian supermarket chains—Delhaize and Colruyt—partnered during the lockdown to deliver groceries to the caregivers in hospitals. This was a bold move, unprecedented in the Belgian retail market! The case I would like to highlight here, however, involves two retailers in Germany.

# Next-level staff collaborations

The concept of employee exchange programs has existed since the nineties among companies with opposing seasonal business cycles. The benefits are avoidance of seasonal layoffs, retention of well-trained staff and increased employee morale. This thinking has yet to expand into other kinds of companies. Collaboration with external partners to share human resources is thus relatively new, despite the fact that it can create opportunities on several levels. During the first lockdown, McDonalds restaurants were closed, their staff unemployed. Knowing that their staff really depend on their wages and often combine several jobs to survive, **McDonalds** collaborated in an unprecedented way with **Aldi** in Germany. The two companies made a staff-sharing deal.[17] This was a highly unusual agreement between companies that had never collaborated before. Aldi was happy to put restaurant staff from McDonalds to work in their stores at short notice. The McDonalds workers could return to their regular jobs once the restaurants reopened.

In the US, something similar happened when three smaller Miami-based brands collaborated: Sedano supermarkets partnered with local restaurant chains Versailles and La Carreta.[18] The independent Hispanic grocery chain said they were looking for 400 extra positions across their stores. This partnership not only provided work for restaurant employees who were facing layoffs because of forced Covid closures, it also demonstrated care for the local community.

These are great examples of how a crisis can lead to an opportunity. You might not need a global pandemic to think about how your staff could exchange ideas or collaborate with others in a win-win situation. Obviously, the transfer agreement must be conducted legally and with the consent of employees. Labour codes are probably not as flexible as one would like them to be and will differ by country, but as Aldi and McDonalds have shown: if you want it to work, it will!

## 4. THE WORLD

Collaboration on sustainability and innovation is becoming a staple on the agenda of business leaders. One cannot cheer loudly enough for brands that join forces in order to rethink or reinvent products or processes in order to take better care of the environment. The truth is, if you don't collaborate on innovation, you'll probably not make it into the next decade! I have leaded several NPD processes and ideation sessions in which we came up with great new concepts.[19] During the ideation sessions, all the members of the innovation team were excited, but fast forward to a couple of months later and most of the ideas had been thrown in the bin. Why? Sure, a bunch of ideas look great when you conceive them, but when you start thinking them over, they often lose their relevance. However, some great product concepts are great product concepts no matter what—but they still never make it simply because the company is unable to produce them.

Fear of asking for help outside the company walls is often too great. The legal contracts needed to work with smaller brands—who would be able to manufacture the products—impose too many constraints on the smaller companies. Most company processes are steered by their corporate legal departments. Innovation teams are obliged to have every move they make checked and double-checked by internal and external lawyers. NDA contracts are the standard in today's collaboration etiquette.[20] This leaves little or no room for creativity, co-creation, collective thinking and collective action—the very principles needed if you want to innovate better, faster and in collaboration with others outside your company walls! Fear of working with other companies is not the only hurdle facing businesses that want to collaborate. The habit of involving universities in the innovation processes is not yet sufficiently widespread. Openness to collaboration with competitors is thin on the

> **People from the board of directors are so completely addicted to the margins of the old normal that they may not survive that new normal.**
>
> **Peter Hinssen, writer**

ground. A different mindset is needed. Your brightest innovation managers will need to go out into the world to find partners with whom they can develop new products and/or services to meet the challenges of tomorrow.

## A paper bottle to join them all

One ground-breaking example in this field was initiated by **Diageo**,[21] an English company with a great portfolio of wine and spirits brands such as Smirnoff and Guinness. They created the world's first ever 100% plastic-free, paper-based spirits bottle made entirely from sustainably sourced wood. This innovation will be launched in 2021 for their Johnnie Walker label. It was created in a partnership with a venture management company.[22] Together they launched Pulpex Limited,[23] a sustainable packaging technology company.

Diageo didn't come up with this innovative bottle for themselves alone—on the contrary! Pulpex have established a partnership with other leading brands such as Unilever and PepsiCo. More brands should step in. This is an act of collaboration on a scale never before witnessed in business. It must have taken a lot of courage and trust on the part of Diageo's management to partner with an external consultancy while allowing their ground-breaking packaging innovation to be used by other big corporations. It is an amazing and beautiful example of how taking care of the planet is best shared with like-minded brands. Together it will go faster, it will be better, it will make more sense. Obviously, sharing the cost of expensive innovation processes comes as a beneficial treat to all!

**Fear of working with other companies is not the only hurdle facing businesses that want to collaborate.**

# Collaboration in a nutshell:

Partnerships on all levels are a source of growth, innovation and legitimacy, and are probably the only way to tackle the growing number of issues ahead of us. Partnerships can be tested on a small scale first to see if they can open profitable doors towards the future, or if they make sense for your type of business. In order to collaborate more effectively, it is necessary to open up company borders on all levels and to review certain processes for better internal collaboration! Trying out a new company structure on a project basis is a good way to test the hurdles before introducing other internal collaboration tools. In short, there has never been a better moment to look over the fence and seek out partnerships with other like-minded folks. Collective thinking and collective action will be key words for your future growth!

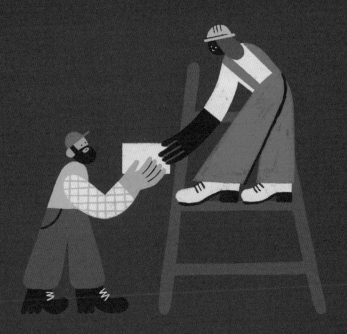

## FREE STUFF YOU CAN DO
## TO ENHANCE COLLABORATION

- Review your individual bonus system and see how you can replace it with teamwork bonuses.

- Set out a clear goal and let your people decide for themselves how and with whom they can collaborate to reach it.

- Ask your staff for ideas and input on how to reorganize, restructure, rethink or reformulate certain flows, products and services.

- Look for like-minded companies and have an open discussion to see whether collaboration in areas such as purchase, logistics, marketing and sales could help both of you.

- Reach out to neighbouring companies to investigate how you can collaborate on tackling issues like waste reduction, mobility, etc.

- Involve schools and/or universities more closely in training programmes, innovation processes and diverse case studies.

# CHAPTER 6

# Why Agility matters

The second Principle that companies need to sharpen is all about speed, reactivity, flexibility, diversification and resilience. It is very important to train your reactivity, as it prepares you for a rapidly changing world. The speed with which these changes become necessary will only increase. We won't go back to business as usual, so you'd best prepare yourself for the next shifts that will be required by economic, ecological, technological and social forces. Movement is key, and responsiveness drives movement. Gone are the days when we could create business and marketing plans a year ahead of time and expect them to be etched in stone. Yes, planning is a necessity, particularly for long-term vision, positioning and innovation, but short-term agility and flexibility are just as important.

## TODAY'S HURDLES

Whenever you want to change something within a company, there are two big hurdles: **people** and processes. Many people don't like change, and they are frightened of changes that might occur in their routines. Changes that might lead to mistakes, that might lead to them getting into trouble. Considered in that light, it is easy to understand why any procedural change is looked at with suspicion. 'Will I be unable to adapt to the new way of doing things, will I lose my job, how will I keep my power and how will I be rewarded?' are among the common fears people express. Demanding a flexible attitude from your staff only works if they trust the organization, if they know that they will not be punished for the try-outs they test. Trust and reliability are very important assets and part of the next Principle. Asking for and demonstrating an agile mindset without trust is difficult.

But your employees are not the only reason why your much-needed organizational change **processes** are unsuccessful. Change processes are often poorly thought out and badly communicated. Some new ways of working are little more than old wine in new bottles. Fancy wording and fancy concepts are unleashed on old hierarchical structures and the management merely hopes for the best for how people will deal with it. Suddenly calling teams 'squads' won't be enough to introduce an agile way of working. Some people might try to boycott newly proposed structures, agile ways of working or changed procedures; there are often good reasons to hold onto the existing ones. In most cases, finding a good balance of what works for the company and its staff while being open and evolving towards a more contemporary organization demands time, an adaptive mindset, compassion and flexibility.

Finally, systems, processes and procedures are often difficult to adapt. Not only can internal procedures be a nightmare to change, the external ones—laws, governmental guidelines, corporate governance rules, checklists and inspection routines—often bring additional headaches of their own. I'm sure that many laws, rules and regulations were made to protect public health or the overall wellbeing of staff. But we have to admit that government regulations are sometimes so out of touch with reality and common sense that they are counterproductive! Laws are lagging behind reality and many companies that try to adapt to new market demands see themselves held back by existing laws and regulations that fall short of actual needs. Hopefully, governments understand that they, too, need to evolve faster to face the challenges ahead.

## TOMORROW'S IMPACT

The way we do business has shifted dramatically, and anyone who isn't flexible enough for the ride will be left behind. Be ready to shift your business model as appropriate, using your customers and their needs as your guide. Chances are that your old habits won't work anymore, so adapt them to create new ways of driving your business forward. A shift in your business model means new opportunities for growth. As mentioned earlier, the world is changing at a pace that is often dazzling. Many things can't be predicted and nobody has a crystal ball, so agility needs to be applied in a manner that fits your organization and at a speed you can handle. Remain true to your company's character and don't force a whole company into a new work mode at once. Look for the people within your company who are more open to change, those characters who are more daring. Start with small teams, build success cases, and slowly but surely transform your organization into one that dares to go faster without cutting corners.

The good news is that agility and an agile mindset can be applied in many ways. Let's look at a few examples of agility that you could apply to stay ahead of the game. Let's see how you could bring agility—and diversification—to the four pillars of the C A R E Principles:

- your people,
- your clients,
- your communities,
- the world.

# 1. YOUR PEOPLE

This chapter is probably the most important for your company to work on, no matter how big or how small. Let's dive into the necessity of it, point by point. As Covid-19 has made perfectly clear, one had always better be prepared for the next normal. Please don't consider this handful of examples to be the only way to demonstrate your resilience—there are many other paths towards becoming a more contemporary, flexible and agile employer.

## THE HYBRID WORK MODE

While the lockdown forced most companies to accelerate digitization so that employees could continue to work from home, the post-Covid world will most likely opt for a hybrid solution. A mix of home and office working will probably give the best results for most companies. Granted, the lockdown also created many benefits. Fewer traffic jams, less commuting stress, cleaner skies and more breathable cities, just to name a few. However, the human need for physical contact remains. Some people became lonely behind their screens; others—especially those with small kids at home—completely lost their work-life balance, as 'work' and 'kids' were always 'on', 24/7. Weekdays and weekends hardly looked any different: there was no commuting time, no dropping the kids at school or sports time. One wonders just how many video calls/meetings one can handle in a day and still stay sane. People need off-screen time now more than ever.

Chances are high that a hybrid model is the way forward. Hybrid can be applied in many ways, and you should develop a model that works best for your company. Hybrid could mean that your staff can do their job whenever it best suits them. This eliminates the 9-to-5 mentality and grants full autonomy to employees to fit work around the rest of their lives, rather than structuring other parts of a weekday around hours logged in an office. To some of you, this may sound like music to your ears, but not every company can function this way. A more common procedure is to designate certain days for in-office meetings and collaboration, and remote days for work involving individual focus. Physical presence might be required for orientations, team building and project kick-offs, but not necessarily for other work.

Frankly, there are many ways of working around a system and setting up a rhythm. Some companies are experimenting with a structure of three days at home combined with two days at the office. Others have given up their offices in favour of a strictly homeworking basis, while others combine homeworking days with satellite offices in co-working spaces across the country, combined with time in the head office. It makes sense to create an organization that offers a flexible way of working, one with a flexible structure and systems that can be accessed from anywhere at any time. Recent studies show that offering your employees flexibility increases productivity and company engagement, two important elements for attracting and keeping talented people.

> ## Success today requires the agility and drive to constantly rethink, reinvigorate, react, and reinvent.
>
> **Bill Gates, entrepreneur**

Whatever hybrid model works best for you and your employees, you also need to consider its potential downsides. Many company systems are not built to be accessed remotely. Whether due to archaic systems or security reasons, it is often impossible to access the right internal document from off-site locations. Furthermore, the division between those who are able to work from home and those who are not exposes socio-economic and racial inequalities.[24] Poor internet access, the demands of parenting and caring, and the lack of roomy homes and outdoor space that make working from home comfortable are just the obvious challenges.[25] Even for those whose homeworking comfort is assured, the right balance between Zoom calls and working time needs to be found as well. I witnessed several clients who spent weekdays from 8 AM until 8 PM in non-stop digital meetings. There was little or no time for a trip to the WC or a lunch break. If we don't achieve a more balanced diet of digital meetings, 'Zoom fatigue' will be the next major Western disease! Finally, don't underestimate the power of physical encounters. Several studies in different fields—from innovation to science—have proven that physical encounters between people and real collaboration help stimulate creativity, serendipity and innovation.

**CASE STUDY**

# Flexibility down under

One nice example of how to deploy a hybrid work mode in an automated, agile way comes from Australia. **Insurance Australia Group** (IAG) uses an app called Switch that gives their call-centre employees credits for taking shifts at high-volume times.[26] Individuals can redeem credits for shifts when there is less demand. 'Contact centres have historically been very structured and inflexible when it comes to people's time,' said Amanda Whiting, IAG executive general manager. 'The benefit of Switch is that it gives our employees more control over their time and work-life balance, while allowing us to manage our business needs. The process of changing shifts has previously been quite manual and often involved several conversations between the employee, their manager, and colleagues. Not only is this time-consuming for the individual, but labour-intensive for the business. The Switch app has automated that process and works in a way that no one needs to justify why they need to make changes and instead can change shifts on their own terms. We recognize that flexibility is different for everyone, which is how Switch really starts to add value,' Whiting continued. Switch is currently used by over 350 IAG call-centre consultants and, since launch, has enabled more than 6,000 shift changes. This flexibility resulted in a 9% increase in employee well-being scores and a 23% decrease in absenteeism.

Updating your work mode is a good start but becoming an agile employer is about more than offering a flexible, hybrid workspace. It also touches deeper societal needs that I'd like to address briefly next.

**DIVERSIFY YOUR STAFF**

There is one change in society that is entirely justified and that is the change in workplace diversity, especially in the Western world. Ethnic, cultural, linguistic and religious fragmentation is a fact, but many companies have yet to adapt to this trend. Let's face it, power today is still largely in the hands of white men. And, so far, history has taught us that male political and business leaders are not always the best at showing they care deeply about inclusion.

Not surprisingly, inclusive leaders are often women—in politics and in business. The countries that best handled the pandemic were mostly led by inclusive and empathic female leaders such as Jacinda Ardern, Prime Minister of New Zealand, Tsai Ing-wen, President of Taiwan, Katrin Jakobsdottir, Prime Minister of Iceland, and Angela Merkel, Chancellor of Germany. Inclusive leaders dare to listen to teams of experts, dare to lean on democratic principles, dare to trust scientists and dare to express their opinion clearly, even if the message is that they aren't entirely sure. Their type of leadership demonstrates that political leaders can be both empathic and strong. Inclusive leadership goes beyond politics; it also counts in business. Every year, the *Financial Times* publishes 'Diversity Leaders',[27] a yearly report on 700 European companies that are assessed on diversity of gender, age, ethnicity, disability and sexual orientation. In the 2019 edition, only one Belgian company appeared in the top 20: Solvay.[28] Is it any coincidence that the CEO of Solvay is Ilham Kadri, a French woman with Moroccan roots? Probably not!

Embracing diversity and inclusion and working towards a gender-balanced workspace is essential for contemporary creative companies. As President of the Belgian Female Association of Marketing, I would like to spend a moment putting the spotlight on **gender equality and female empowerment**. In the Gender Gap Index 2020,[29] the World Economic Forum announced that it will take another 99.5 years to reach gender parity at today's speed! Most companies have been working on their gender equality objectives for years: through internal diversity and gender equality programmes, through quotas and initiatives designed to spot and help women break through the glass ceiling. Reality has shown that it doesn't work.

Why aren't there more women at the C-level? The reasons for this are diverse and complex.[30] An unconscious bias on the part of men is certainly one of the reasons. Men can't help it, but they simply don't know what it is to be a woman. If you don't believe it and you want a glimpse of what it's like to be a woman in a man's world, have a look at the French romantic movie *Je ne suis pas un homme facile*.[31] It may not be an Oscar winner, but the movie definitely has a few eye-opening scenes that give you an idea of how the world would look if women acted like men and vice versa.

Both women and men also tend to overestimate men and underestimate women. History—which was written largely by men—tells us that men are leaders, so people continue to have that expectation. Women also shoot themselves in the foot by not daring to grab that promotion because they're afraid they won't be able to fill a larger pair of shoes. This is an attitude not many men share. Most men would just take the promotion and deal with the issues when and if they turned up. Combine this with the old-boy network attitude of men helping men, and you understand why the battle has not yet been won. Women need to create their own smart female networks. As President of FAM, I try to create awareness among female marketers, encouraging them to act and think differently, to challenge traditional role patterns and expectations. Change is slow, but progress is made.

> Be fast, have no regrets. If you need to be right before you move, you will never win.
>
> **Dr Michael J. Ryan, executive director World Health Organization**

Why progress is so slow is anybody's guess, as there are numerous studies and companies that demonstrate the benefits of gender diversity.[32] With more women at the top, your company will function better, will be more creative, will innovate better and faster. Finally—and this may be the one argument that convinces even the most hard-boiled of traditional executives—more women in positions of power will make you more money and more profit!

Diversity in the workplace means that a company's workforce includes people of varying gender, age, religion, race, ethnicity, cultural background, sexual orientation, language, education, ability, etc. Making your workforce more diverse is not only necessary if you want to evolve towards being a more inclusive and contemporary employer, it is also required if you hope to understand your customers. Your target group has become diverse, so how can you address their needs if you have no clue how they think and act? Your company should mirror society, and the reality of most companies today is far removed from this ideal. Let's tune in to one of the most famous Chinese companies, Alibaba, and read how founder Jack Ma is supporting women on all levels.

**CASE STUDY**

## Women take command in China

I must admit, many things come to mind when I think of China, but female leadership is not one of them! **Alibaba**, however, is demonstrating how employing and empowering women can give you a real competitive advantage.[33] Founder Jack Ma claims that women are the secret to his company's success. Women are well-represented within Alibaba: one-third of Alibaba's executive positions are held by women. In addition, half of the sellers on its gigantic Tmall and Taobao marketplaces are women. Tmall is an open, business-to-consumer platform in China enabling brands from all over the globe to sell directly to Chinese citizens. They have over 500 million registered customers and over 50% market share in Asia. Jack Ma even goes so far as to claim that men need to be on their guard, as women's perseverance and attention to detail enable them to outperform men,

especially now, in the era of robotics and machine learning.

Alibaba Group's belief in women goes beyond hiring them and giving them a platform on which to trade. In 2015 they also launched a Global Conference on Women and Entrepreneurship. They did this to jumpstart a conversation among women on empowerment and personal fulfilment as entrepreneurs, leaders, policymakers and role models for future generations. Their latest gathering in 2019 went global, with the presence of Rihanna and Melinda Gates among other female role models. Jack Ma stated that 'achieving gender equality is the goal he cares for the most'. Making campaigns like 'the world she made' or actively supporting STEM education for girls are just some examples of Alibaba's efforts to stimulate women's empowerment.

## 2. YOUR CLIENTS

It's great if you have been working on your
internal organization, have developed a
fab internal culture, or have been named
Employer of the Year. Those are all amazing
achievements, and I congratulate you.
The C A R E Principles, however, are not
meant for internal use only—they also face
the outside world, starting with your clients.
As we examine ways to develop more
agility towards your external stakeholders,
here are a few points to think about:

- your target groups,
- your products/services,
- your distribution, and
- how you communicate your offer.

### TARGET GROUPS

I agree that every company today has already gone through the exercise of
looking for new target groups. Still, I want to challenge and inspire you to redo
this exercise and try to look at it from a different point of view. Most brands
have either a generic product or service for a 'Tintin' target group, meaning
everybody from seven to seventy-seven years old, or a very specific target
group—like business-to-business machine park owners. Whatever your situation,
it is important for your brand to stay true to its core target group. If you develop
a young hipster brand, it will feel untrue to your core group if you sell in
mainstream shops. If you target an elderly male population, it will be tough to
reach new customers on Instagram: the average Instagrammer is female, aged
24–34.[34] You get the point. It is of utmost importance to keep your brand
experience as sharp as you can in order for consumers to identify with it. Still,
I would like to challenge you to rethink your target group by sharing an example
of a Dutch hard discounter who did it in a surprising but highly beneficial way.

# A Dutch discounter with a different approach

A great example of expanding your target group without losing touch with your core, comes from **Zeeman**, one of my personal favourite Dutch brands! In the retail textile market, there has not been much positive going on lately. Many brands have gone bankrupt or are struggling to survive. Yet Zeeman has been on a consistent path of brand differentiation and growth since 2015. Back then they launched a daring strategy in their retail segment by quitting the weekly circular. Instead, they increased their investment in TV and online media.

In addition to taking a daring media approach, they had a close look at their product offer. They decided to create a limited number of remarkable products a couple of times a year. They launched and promoted these limited editions at atypical moments. They eschewed extra advertising around traditional retail moments such as Easter, Christmas or Valentine's Day, but splashed out on full media budgets for limited edition festival collections for youngsters, or specialty items like bridal gowns.

Then they began to explain, openly and transparently, about their quality and price setting. They created basic but appealing advertising campaigns, found their own tone of voice, used it consistently over time in all their touchpoints and showcased their real clients in most advertising campaigns. This consistent approach—in a declining market—proved they were right. In 2018 they won a Gold Effie in the Netherlands with stunning results:

- Quality perception climbed in three years from 25.7% to 64.4%.
- They grew at a rate of double the market average.

In 2019,[35] even though they closed several shops, they continued their growth with 5% compared to 2018 and had a €639 million turnover. To round out this impressive growth story, they continue their sustainability efforts by producing 25% of their textiles in eco-friendly materials.

I am a big fan of this brand, and not only for their winning strategy in such compelling times. They turned a 'cheap' brand into a 'fun' brand for fashionistas and influencers with their fan collections. A limited edition collection of 'wannahave' items will sell out in a blink. This is another one of their merits. Getting massive press coverage and attracting new target groups—such as fiancées with a wedding dress for €29.99, or hipsters with a sneaker for €12.99 or a perfume called 'lucht' for €4.99—they always seem to reach a different target group each time, despite the fact that they didn't invest much in their in-store shopping experience.

Knowing that the fashion and influencer gang lives and shops digitally, they were probably right to focus on the online experience first. Having said that, they have proven that they know, understand and act upon people's needs. Not only do they offer appealing products, they also launch them with exactly the right strategy. From influencers to young brides, everybody became a fan of Zeeman. But as a true gamechanger in the retail industry, they are also an example of how to take care of their

communities. Where the average payment of suppliers in this industry is 120 days, they have made it a habit to pay their suppliers within fourteen days. This is unprecedented in the industry and taking this much care of their suppliers, some of whom they have been collaborating with for more than forty years, is pretty rare! One nice side effect of this caring attitude: during the pandemic, it gave them a head start when shops reopened, as they received their deliveries first from their loyal suppliers.

So think again: What does the future of your main target group look like? Is there room to rethink your product/service and aim at a new potential target group? Are you in a declining market? If so, can you look for new target groups? Of course you can—but learn from the best: get under the skin of that target group before you launch. You only get one chance to do it right!

## PRODUCTS/SERVICES

Most products and services on the market today exist simply because somebody came up with an idea and found a way to produce it. However, better understanding your target groups and really getting to know their ins and outs by studying consumer behaviour can bring more success than looking at what your machines are capable of producing. Creating a flexible and adaptive product portfolio has been done many times. Adapting your products could mean basic things, such as changing packaging, formats, shapes or sizes to fit other consumption moments. But looking at changed consumer behaviour, turning your products into services or responding to people's psychological needs can all be brilliant entries to kickstarting new product development. As we are living in a tech-driven, digital age, I'll give you an example of a product that was invented in 1835 but has now become hotter than hot in the US!

**CASE STUDY**

## Mirror, mirror on the wall

Since its invention in Germany in 1835, the mirror has been made in all shapes and sizes, but it took until 2018 for an American dancer to revolutionize this product and turn it into a digital million-dollar experience! If you haven't already heard of **Mirror**,[36] a start-up founded by Brynn Putnam, you should have: it was sold for $500 million in 2020 to the Canadian brand Lululemon, a yoga-inspired, technical athletic apparel company for both women and men. Celebrities like Reese Witherspoon, Alicia Keys and Ellen DeGeneres have openly expressed their admiration for this product.

The Mirror sells for $1495—and yes, it's large and pretty, but aesthetics is not the reason their fans are willing to put down this amount of money for it. No, with the Mirror comes a subscription format. Again, at quite a price: the cheapest deal is $42/month! What does the deal include? Well,

Mirror is a home fitness tool giving you access to streaming sessions in all kinds of activities, from meditation to kickboxing. You can also 'hire' a personal coach through your Mirror and get a live lesson with a personal trainer who gives you directions through your Mirror. But there is more to its smartness than good looks and interactivity. First, it is an ideal object for people living in small spaces, as it doesn't take up much space. It can stand alone, or it can be hung and has a simple mirror function for when you are not working out. Secondly, next to the fact that almost everybody uses a mirror in their house, this one reminds you to train your body every time you look at it!

Mirror and other interactive fitness companies, such as Peloton,[37] which gives interactive lessons on a stationary bike, had tens of thousands of subscribers in 2020 and has seen their business accelerate during the pandemic. The fact that gyms had to close for long periods definitely gave a boost to the home fitness rage, but the success of Mirror goes beyond Covid-19. Mirror is a vessel for content. Pair the device with the Mirror app and you have access to thousands of workout sessions, available on demand. Professional trainers appear onscreen against a pure black background to lead you through classes that run somewhere between fifteen minutes and an hour. You can work out to Mirror's curated playlists or your own Spotify account, and adjust the volume of both the music and the instructor's voice. You can train your body whenever you want and not just when the gym classes are scheduled, or when your gym is open! When you follow the live classes, a feeling of community is created by sharing the names of the other participants.

Finally, Mirror also can monitor your heart rate.

Future health applications will surely follow. As it is a location-based app, you can bet that they will soon partner with organic food and beverage companies to deliver a healthy shake after your workout. They also launched a digital service offering you the lessons on any other device, making it possible to stay hooked to their streaming content while on holiday or away from your home. Mirror is definitely more than just a product: it is becoming an in-home media content experience, and its makers will continue to adapt Mirror's functionalities and roles in the life of its owners to remain a relevant and active part of their lives. Did I get your hopes up? Sorry—so far, Mirror is only available in the US!

## DISTRIBUTION

Looking at your distribution channels differently and rethinking your distribution strategy is an exercise that certainly needs your attention. Having multiple ways to distribute your product/service is definitely a smart way to protect yourself against any setback. So many brands saw their sales plummet because retail channels, shops, restaurants and bars were forced to close during the first corona wave. The Covid-19 pandemic appears to be accelerating deglobalization, with export figures dropping massively. Heavily depending on one or two channels or relying mainly on one or two countries abroad can cause a lot of stress and financial hassle. Most companies tend to copy their competitors as an easy way of getting more revenue, and this can certainly work in some cases. But it is also smart to look outside your own category and see how other sectors are selling their products. Adapting existing models by tweaking them slightly to work for your products can be an easy way to reach different target groups and generate more revenue.

**CASE STUDY**

# The billion dollar vending machine

The Belgian online jewellery brand **Billion Avenue**[38] stepped outside their usual digital sales channels and developed a vending machine. This well-branded offline pop-up made its appearance in carefully curated locations where a new target group could be reached. In this case, the vending machine popped up during the summer at The Guest Store, a high-end, Belgian brand concept store in Knokke, a chic seaside resort. Since this successful test, they have installed several vending machines in different cities. It worked, catering to the desire for 'instant indulgence' of their young target group, who want to buy fancy earrings 'right here, right now'!

Rethinking your distribution model is not always a walk in the park. It might demand a totally different approach to the way you think today. You'll probably need different staff, as every new channel has its specific needs and nuances that need to be carefully taken into account and catered to accordingly. It can demand serious investment. It will definitely cost you money to learn the tricks and tips from each new distribution channel you decide to try out. Too many companies today are afraid of testing things out on a scale that is too small, leaving little opportunity to let things grow. Business cases are a necessary tool in estimating the risk of any idea, but successful innovations often happen by chance. Think of Barco, for instance, which launched Clickshare, a tiny screen-sharing device that was originally designed in 2009 as an accessory for their projectors. Today, it has become an easy-to-use wireless presentation and conferencing tool that is now installed in more than half a million meeting rooms. Barco's company solutions division now generates 35%[39] of its total revenue and continues to grow. Barco's CEO admitted that it wasn't an easy decision for the board to invest millions in a new technology that, at the time, seemed to be a niche business for an enterprise primarily oriented towards cinema projectors, but it turned out to be the right move. Like Barco, you'll need to be prepared to learn, fail, rethink, adjust and reboot any innovation—but this is precisely the mode your company will need to be in from now on.

## COMMUNICATION

A reactive and flexible mindset in communication is all about closely monitoring and understanding your target groups. Some brands manage to keep pace with their target groups, carefully studying all available data about them. However, many brands are still stuck in a classic type of content creation and seem stuck in a very traditional relationship with their agencies as well. Briefings are made slowly and mainly internally, like a new product launch. All too often, media and creative agencies are still briefed separately, and depending on the quality of these agencies, one of them usually takes the lead and rarely collaborates openly with the other to come up with the best possible idea for the brand. Although any marketer today understands the power of social and digital, many still use their 'offline methods and timings' to steer their digital content creators.

The problem is not restricted to brand owners, either. Many digital and social agencies make stereotypical and predictable online content that is shared in a planned and structured way through platforms such as Hootsuite or MeetEdgar. Social media management tools definitely enable you to automate, analyse and better control your social media accounts. These apps can post the same updates on all your social accounts, schedule future updates and help you find the most appropriate and effective content to post and the best times at which to post it. But they often make content predictable: just look at all the brands that use the 'top topical agenda' to make posts around typical 'moments': International Coffee Day, Halloween or Valentine's Day. While this structures your content, it also lacks the day-to-day, native posting approach that leaves more room to connect with your audiences in a more 'live' and 'right here, right now' mode.

Understandably, many marketing departments cannot ask their staff to be online 24/7 and to adapt and improvise on a daily basis. But the rewards for those who can are considerable. A famous brand like Nike is not only an award-winning advertising champion, it is also a social media king. With a total of 318 social media profiles catering to a multitude of products and geolocations, Nike is one of the most followed brands online. Nike uses all major platforms: Facebook, Twitter, YouTube, Pinterest and LinkedIn. The brand diversified their online presence by creating separate pages for its products catering to different target audiences. They have it all: the budgets, the products, the influencers, the athletes and the best agencies in the world to turn it all into top creative content. Granted, it's Nike! But there are other giant brands that have all of the above, yet Nike still makes the difference with the speed and agility they apply to their communication—a lesson that even those with smaller budgets and fewer staff can learn from. They are almost always one of the first brands to react to whatever is happening in the world, and they have had a feeling for what goes on in their communities for decades. When Nike released their commercial 'For once, don't do it'[40] five days after the death of George Floyd, or launched the 'Mamba forever'[41] commercial and movement after the fatal accident of basketball player Kobe Bryant, it was clear that no global brand is as fast as they are to express their beliefs and culture, to showcase what they stand for.

## Leaders are talking the talk about empathy, but are failing to walk the walk!

**Business Solvers**

Nike is clearly a brand that understands how to be close to their audience, whether that audience is black, white, gay, straight or gender neutral. Their unusual combination of agility and empathy is pretty impressive. They show they understand the grief of the black communities, the sacrifices it takes to be a top athlete, the hurt it causes the rest of us to start to run. They dig deep into their clients' psychological needs, fears and dreams and translate them into award-winning campaigns. They have done this for decades, and hopefully they will continue to do so for decades to come. But I can already hear you thinking: 'Not another marketing book that holds up Nike, always Nike, as an example … I heartily agree; therefore, the case study on agility in communication involves a different brand, a brand you might have heard of—probably because they were in big trouble. Read on to find out how Chipotle managed to turn the tide of negative publicity through agile communication.

**CASE STUDY**

# Chipotle cleans up its act

Chipotle[42] is an American chain of fast casual restaurants in the US, UK, Canada, Germany and France specializing in Mexican tacos and mission burritos. In 2016, fifty-five people were infected with E. coli bacteria after having eaten at this chain. Since then, the brand's recovery has been slow, despite many investments in food safety measures. A study conducted two years later[43] showed that people were still afraid to eat there. How did communication help them turn the tide?

First came a new CEO, Brian Niccol, who previously generated impressive growth at Taco Bell with creative marketing and wild new menu items, such as the Naked Chicken Chalupa.[44] He quickly installed the idea of variety in the menu, something the chain didn't have before, rolling out new, limited-time offers and products with funky names. Secondly, he brought breakfast and alcohol to the table. This experiment around daypart strategies was successful too, creating traffic in the restaurants from morning to evening. Extra investment in food safety, sustainable food, reduced waste and digital sales, among other things, were also part of the declining

brand's big turnaround process. But Niccol was hired mainly because he was responsible for some of Taco Bell's most iconic ads, which helped make the chain's fame. A new approach to marketing and rapid testing of new menu items through social media helped the chain get back on its feet.

CEO Niccol and his marketing team understood that for Chipotle to remain in business, they could not just repeat the tricks he pulled off at Taco Bell. Following the chain's target group meant following them into the rapidly changing world of popular social media platforms. After Facebook came Instagram, then Snapchat and TikTok took the world by storm. Chipotle morphed into a triumphant lifestyle brand on TikTok. The Chipotle team decided to create a presence on TikTok after seeing their brand repeatedly mentioned by users of the app when a Chipotle Instagram video of an employee flipping a lid over a burrito bowl made it onto the platform. They launched their account with the lid flipping video and challenged followers to shoot their own tricks. For National Avocado Day, they capitalized on a popular internet dance hit by Dr Jean, an American teacher who became famous for her children's learning songs: the so-called 'guacamole song' from 2010 has over 36 million views![45] Chipotle capitalized on a song and dance that every Gen Alpha American grew up with. Its #GuacDance challenge, which kicked off in July 2020, has already had more than a billion views. The campaign is TikTok's highest-performing branded challenge in the US so far. The online promotion resulted in Chipotle's biggest guacamole day ever, with more than 800,000 sides of the condiment served in all restaurants.[46] A smart move from a brand that understood how to engage culturally with Generations Z and Alpha.[47] Today, Chipotle has managed to garner 1.3 million followers on TikTok in less than a year.

One of the secrets to Chipotle's success is their dedicated team of cultural researchers, referred to as 'culture hunters'. The culture hunters are curious Internet users who gauge what customers are posting about and what online trends are most popular, information that Chipotle spins into social campaigns. A diverse team in Chipotle's marketing department, including people from Gen Z, has been a key ingredient in establishing a genuine brand personality. They do this not only by sharing culturally appealing content, but also by showing the people behind the brand telling real life stories without taking themselves too seriously, and by adding a touch of humour and humanity to everything they do. They don't want to feel like an advertiser, said Tressie Lieberman, Chipotle's vice president of digital, and that is probably the most amazing advice she can give any brand that wants to conquer the heart of future generations!

Using the power of each particular channel and sharing real content that resonates with your target group is another lesson to remember. Following, understanding and translating the online trends that capture customers' attention in an agile way is the future of communication for many brands.

## 3. YOUR COMMUNITIES

Taking care of your communities in an agile way means reacting to constant change in ways that will benefit those with whom you come into contact. Your communities may be very diverse: your shareholders, a founder or owner of the company, the board of directors, your local government or mayor, your suppliers or tenants ... This is just a handful of communities with which your brand might be in contact on a regular basis. Let's face it, taking care of them has

never been the number one priority of any company in the business models we've been accustomed to until now. This looks set to change as stakeholder capitalism gains an increasing foothold in the world. It's never too soon to look around and reflect, to find new ways to build a long-lasting, sustainable relationship with the communities you deal with regularly.

Taking care of your communities is more immediately and easily applied in the shift towards collaboration, reliability and empathy; in any of these efforts, an agile mindset can help you rethink your relationship for the better. A Brussels hotel offers a splendid example. The hospitality sector was massively affected by the coronavirus and is still suffering all over the world, but one hotel owner decided to pivot towards his local community rather than helplessly stand by and wring his hands.

**CASE STUDY**

## A hotel with a heart

Nicolas Jancen inherited **Hotel Galia**, the only hotel located in the Marolles, a working-class neighbourhood in Brussels.[48] His grandparents came to Belgium as Russian refugees in 1917 and never forgot how well they were received in their adopted country. It was probably this recognition of solidarity that flows through Jancen's veins. When Brussels refugee camps were closed due to corona restrictions, he decided to open up the doors of his hotel and welcome them to sleep in a clean bed, to be able to take a shower and live a decent life while in exile. In collaboration with a diverse group of civic volunteers, organizations such as BXL Refugees, Doctors without Borders, governmental institutions and pro bono lawyers, they managed to keep over 100 refugees off the streets during the first lockdown. As soon as the news spread through the city, several taxi companies, local stores and civilians brought food, clothes, and other necessary amenities to help these emigrants. Nicolas has only positive feelings about the sudden change in the purpose of his hotel. He regrets that he was unable to host more people but affirms that it was the right thing to do. He has no idea what the future will bring for his hotel business, but I am sure he will adapt swiftly whenever another move feels necessary.

## 4. THE WORLD

Adapting to a rapidly changing world is something that more and more companies understand. No company—large or small, start-up or centenarian—stands alone. The globalized world is interconnected, and even if we seem to live in a moment of global standstill due to the limits on travel recently imposed by the pandemic, there is no doubt that globalization will continue. The butterfly effect has been proven.[49] Given the complexity of environmental change, many companies have started rethinking their business model, product offer, production processes, etc. in order to take better care of the planet. Using technology, robotization and innovations to future-proof your company by making it faster, better and more sustainable is the next level to strive for.

Many brands have started accelerating their sustainability efforts with initiatives that can only be supported and cheered, as the world will need a joint effort to tackle the climate change issues we are facing. However, the next example that I have chosen is not a brand. This was a deliberate choice. Instead, I have chosen a city, a city that understood long before others that it needed to take planned, coordinated action to protect the future and well-being of its citizens. As city marketing has become such an important tool in tourism, you might be inclined to agree that cities should start acting like brands. Copenhagen understood that long before many other cities. Read on to find out how Copenhagen will become the first carbon-neutral city in the world!

**CASE STUDY**

# Copenhagen cuts down to level up

When the European commission president, Ursula von der Leyen, placed the European Green Deal back on the table in 2020, she knew it was ambitious. Lowering carbon emissions by 55% by 2030 will only be possible if Europeans completely and collectively transform their lives, work and living situations. How member countries will go on to realize this ambitious plan is still uncertain, but I love the example of **Copenhagen,** the city that refused to wait for a big European vision or plan. In 2005 they decided to become the first carbon-neutral city in the world by 2025, and they're on a mission to achieve this admirable plan! Copenhagen was one of the first cities in the world to understand that it needed to become better and greener—in the first place for its own inhabitants. Lowering their $CO_2$ emissions, creating better bike lanes, greener transport and sustainable urban development are

just a few of the initiatives they took. Mayor Ritt Bjerregaard reckoned in 2009 that the plan had cost them a pretty penny at the time, but he and other political stakeholders also understood that it was an investment with good returns. Financially speaking, the return is yet to come. In terms of health, performance and wellbeing, for all those who live, work and visit Copenhagen, the return is already tangible.

Over 70% of the world's $CO_2$ emissions come from cities. Cities hold the key to the global climate challenge. Copenhagen took the lead with their Climate Plan, as they cared for their city, their inhabitants, their country and the world. Although this book focuses on brands, any city today should think, act and plan like a brand. Only when cities are well governed— which means only when they think ahead and adapt to the changing needs of their inhabitants and the challenges they face—will they remain relevant. What I love about Copenhagen's approach is that they announced from the start that their plan was dynamic. The city's white paper, which can be downloaded free of charge, states that 'not all initiatives will look exactly as they are described here. We are part of a changing world, and national and global laws also influence our climate'.[50] Copenhagen not only proved to have great vision, it also demonstrated the flexible and agile mindset needed to reach their goals. I can't wait to go back and test a car that runs on wind energy and visit the new science centre to learn more about climate education!

**Diversify your staff: your target group has become diverse, so how can you address their needs if you have no clue how they think and act?**

## Agility in a nutshell:

There are many more fields in which you can introduce an agile mindset and create a company that reacts faster and better. Think about how your customer service, project management or procurement can become more flexible. There are endless possibilities to look at your organization and see where agility leads in terms of getting a better grasp on the rapidly changing world. Nothing is written in stone or established forever.

## FREE STUFF YOU CAN DO
## TO BECOME MORE AGILE

- Hire someone of a different gender, age, ethnicity, disability or sexual orientation; it costs no extra money and may earn you more in the long run.

- Look at businesses outside your own sector; learning from their procedures can be a cheap and easy way to install more agility in your own processes.

- Ask your fans, community and social media followers about certain options, new products or services you are thinking of launching; it can be done quickly and easily. It won't replace an in-depth market research project, but it can give you enough insights to move on with a particular project.

- Outsource what you can't afford. Building an agile e-commerce site from scratch with an impeccable user experience can be a long and expensive venture. Don't be afraid to rely on existing platforms such as Shopify, Wix, Magento and many others. For a small monthly fee, you can focus on your business without getting lost in technology, security and mobile responsiveness issues.

- Communicate with the young. If you don't have money to hire culture hunters, talk to your kids or teenagers on a regular basis and ask them what they eat, who they follow online, what the latest buzz or challenge is about and see how you can learn from their insights.

# CHAPTER 7

# Why Reliability is crucial

Being a respectful, trustworthy brand that
values integrity and honesty is probably
something that all companies believe in.
In the list of values most companies develop,
integrity is nearly always mentioned. So why
is reliability part of the C A R E Principles?

## TODAY'S HURDLES

There was a time when reliability mainly applied to the factual aspects of a company: offering a reliable product, having a good reputation with your clients, scoring high in the ranks of best employer lists, having trustworthiness as one of your company values ... all of these things build your company's reliability factor. For decades now, trust has been built through marketing. Creating a decent product, adding a robust brand identity, showcasing it through a trustworthy brand image and using storytelling to enhance your great achievements.

It is important to understand that building a reputation today is not done like in the old days. For decades trust was built through marketing and advertising. Trust was basically built through carefully manicured actions, campaigns and images. But let's face it, your brand image was often far from reality. That is okay as that was the way the whole world used to build a trustworthy brand image! We all participated in this picture perfect life! However today, the morality of brands is questioned so trust has to be won in a different way. But that is not the only reason why a reliable reputation has to be built in a different way. A multitude of other things have happened too.

First, an increase in technology, data and connectivity resulted in audiences having higher expectations and lower attention spans when it came to content. Filtering out your manicured brand content is simply a matter of daily habit for many people. Secondly, today's consumers have more choices, more power and more information at their command when they make fast, connected decisions about how they really think and feel about your brand.

> If there is one thing you need in times of crisis it is trust. Trust in your employees.
>
> **Jonathan Berte, CEO Robovision**

Audiences have a habit of checking social (83%), search (73%), and news sites and apps (77%) at least once or multiple times daily,[51] which means your company is no longer people's sole source of brand reliability. Your company exists in an exposed, public space, where people will dig into your brand on all levels. Why?

Well, unfortunately, many companies have proven to be unreliable, despite their manicured marketing efforts. Too many examples can be found—in all industries, worldwide. Remember Dieselgate, when auto manufacturers tried to game emissions standards?[52] Or think of the aggressive climate lobbying sponsored by big oil firms.[53] The food industry also let us down on several occasions: Remember how Toblerone thought it could outsmart consumers in 2016 by cutting back the weight and design of its iconic triangular bar?[54] More recently, high-profile examples of companies praised as paragons that turned out to be anything but have further shaken public trust—in companies and the government bodies responsible for regulating them. The German payment processing firm Wirecard comes to mind, as does the Belgian fashion group FNG, both of which created black holes in their accounts, misleading their staff, their clients, their auditors and the whole world. The list goes on and on: Exxon misled Americans for decades on climate change.[55] Both Monsanto and Bayer kept insisting that their weedkiller Round Up was safe rather than carcinogenic.[56] And Hertz attempted to sell one billion dollar in stock despite being bankrupt until financial bodies managed to pressure them into stopping.[57]

**The most valuable business commodity is trust.**

**Richard Branson, founder Virgin Group**

Citizen trust in businesses is particularly critical for tech and media companies. Data breaches, and the startling revelation that big tech companies were listening into our private lives through Alexa, Skype calls or Google assistant, haven't helped them build an open, transparent and trusting relationship with consumers. Europe has tried to protect its citizens through the GDPR laws, but let's be honest—the vast majority of companies haven't been fined or sanctioned for not doing a better job of protecting our data. And even tech giants like Amazon have had to deal with major data breaches. Media outlets spreading fake news or deliberately opting not to remove content that might lead to violence[58]—even if that content comes from a US president—have not helped the reputation and trustworthiness of these brands.

I'll not go any deeper into dishonest brands and dishonest people, as they don't deserve any more attention. They screwed up—that's a fact. Many companies stumble in their draconian search for growth and short-term profit. Ingrained short-term thinking is a near-universal phenomenon, unfortunately, and will probably always exist. However, consumer behaviour has shifted. People have become marketing savvy; the sheer amount of information at their fingers is breathtaking, and their respect for brands has taken on new dimensions. You might want to start adjusting to the fact that this is not your grandfather's reliability. Hopefully, society and citizens will become savvy enough to reject this type of delusive leadership and reckless behaviour in future.

## TOMORROW'S IMPACT

It is time to be open, transparent, honest and authentic. It is time to dare to admit that perfection doesn't exist. It is time to admit that we are all in the midst of a non-stop process of transformation, and that this process will always have a few blind corners somewhere. That's okay. Even the biggest brands in the industry today are now willing to admit that they have weak spots. Of course they have, as do we all! The important lesson about reliability is not to try and cover up your mistakes. Talk about them openly and sincerely. Dare to say what went wrong and how you will try to solve it.

Trust is not built overnight and cannot be created in an executive meeting room. Trust needs to be earned. It is a bottom-up process that starts with receiving trust from your employees. It is an inside-out process that acts on many different levels towards all your stakeholders: your employees, your community, your customers, your suppliers, your vendors, your local government. Trust comes in many shapes and forms and will be linked to ethical and transparency drivers.

If you are a trustworthy company, for instance, it is not really ethical to expect your suppliers to accept a 120-day payment term, a practice still applied today at many multinationals. Despite having all kinds of diversity, sustainability and supply-chain transparency plans, many companies still ask their suppliers to deliver goods to them upfront and only pay them four months later. Now that is not what most people would consider ethical, nor does it signal a trustworthy relationship. Introducing ethical drivers in these turbulent times—with governments, media and other institutions under pressure, and with an explosion of troll factories that fabricate fake news and deep fakes—will become crucial.

There is, however, a silver lining and an opportunity for companies to do better. There is room for companies to step in and become a reliable factor in people's lives. With less trust in government and media, people expect brands to step in and help solve the issues facing the world. Today, people express as much trust in businesses as they do in NGOs.[59] Trust has become a factor people value almost as highly as product benefits. Each day, consumers are more aware that they vote with their wallet. So it matters how you act. It matters how you show you care. It matters how reliable you are!

> Trust is earned in the smallest of moments. It is earned not through heroic deeds, or even highly visible actions, but through paying attention, listening, and gestures of genuine care and connection.
>
> Brené Brown, research professor & author

Business leaders all over the world have started to realize this. In the 'Decade to deliver' report from the UN and Accenture,[60] it's fascinating to read the number of CEOs who are aware that they can be part of the change needed and who want to contribute to the seventeen Global Goals set out in the report,[61] such as climate action, poverty reduction, gender equality, and so on. Of the CEOs that participated, 76% say citizen **trust** will be critical to business competitiveness in their industry in the next five years.

This shift in awareness is an important first step in creating trust. Let's return to the backbone of the C A R E model and see what reliability can mean for your people, your clients, your communities and the world.

## 1. YOUR PEOPLE

To build trust, companies can start by better articulating their societal or higher purpose. First they can define their value to society and see how they can implement this internally. Having a higher purpose is no longer a marketing domain—it's a top-down process that starts on the inside, with the company leadership. Convincing your employees that you are a trustworthy brand comes first. The Trust Barometer states that 92% of employees expect their CEO to lead and speak out about societal challenges. CEOs should take the lead and will be seen as agents of change in society. They could become the rock stars of tomorrow, and their reliability score and trustworthiness will give them more power than their economic value. They will not only lead their enterprise; they will also represent the loudest voice from within the industry and show their stakeholders—and not just their shareholders—what they care about and how valuable it is to them.

How can you become a trustworthy employer? And how does this reflect on your brand's reputation? Let's have a closer look at a small, family owned engineering office and learn from them how simple it can be.

**CASE STUDY**

## Jonckheere keeps it quiet

Koen Jonckheere[62] is the second generation in a small, family run engineering firm based in Bruges, Belgium. Since receiving the Liantis Award[63] for welfare and prevention, he is often asked by other companies how he established a climate of care and trust for employees and what effect it has had on his staff.

For Koen, it is pretty straightforward. To avoid distractions that might lead to mistakes—something an engineering firm must avoid at all costs—he knew he had to protect his people's focus. An engineering bureau cannot make mistakes. Any mistake could have devastating consequences, not only for their reputation, but also for clients ranging from local governments, cities and architects to other engineering entities. The key to giving his staff the peace of mind they need to work accurately is a set of basic 'rules':

- Library hour: the first two hours of the day are spent in total silence. Colleagues work in silence. Nobody talks about the weekend, and department leaders are not asked for explanations or bothered with other questions.
- No meetings can be scheduled at the start of the day, so the day starts with focus on the job.
- Emails are dispatched automatically according to the job and only sent to the people involved in the job, nobody else.
- No needless 'email cc' culture.
- Emails are read twice a day only; for the rest of the day, the mailboxes remain closed.
- Emails are often not answered until the person responsible has all the information needed to communicate one overall answer to the client instead of answering bit by bit.
- People are asked to use email as an informational tool and for no other reason.
- Meetings are held to exchange information. If too many emails or calls are made afterwards, it means the meeting wasn't sufficiently well prepared, or that it was planned at the wrong moment. This way, people

are challenged to work in the most time-efficient way possible.
- No mobile phones are allowed during business hours, so no private messages or surfing disturb working hours.
- At 4:30 PM the office closes and the employees can go home, leaving them time to take care of their personal lives.
- No work is taken home.

This unique work policy might seem harsh and old fashioned to some, but it has proven to work well in fostering the concentration needed by these architects, mathematicians and engineers. Taking care of employees by introducing these simple rules didn't cost anything (other than the automated email system). The fact that it has led to more accuracy, less stress and fewer burnouts positioned Jonckheere as an attractive employer for young engineers who value their work-life balance. The fact that it is carefully watched over by their boss is an added bonus. Taking care of staff by giving them more time to focus on their jobs has given Jonckheere a solid and trustworthy reputation. A simple but great way of building reliability, both inside the company—as people know exactly what they are getting into when they sign a job contract with Jonckheere—but also with clients and suppliers, as it bodes well for a steady, trustworthy relationship.

## 2. YOUR CLIENTS

As mentioned earlier, nobody is perfect and neither are companies. People are looking at brands and asking them to do the right thing, but consumer demands are often unrealistic and hard to fulfil. We also see that many consumers are capricious, and their behaviour is often contradictory. Youngsters who participate in climate protests seem to have no moral issues when they order a $3 T-shirt from the Chinese e-commerce site Shein, for instance. But young people are not the only ones guilty of contradictory behaviour—we can all experience pitfalls and behave illogically. Companies now have mountains of data to help them better understand their clients. What is important to your clients? How can you gain their trust? How can you help them in their lives? How can you accompany them throughout their lives? Companies must—on a day-to-day level—continue to improve their ethical behaviour and remain reliable on all levels for their clients. Daring to communicate with your customers openly and transparently is the only road towards the future.

Like so many other things, building trust is a long-term project, not a sprint. Remember, trust is hard to gain but easy to lose. Young brands need to build trust from scratch; established brands have a heritage they can rely on. In our next case study, we encounter a museum that didn't take its imperial heritage for granted!

**CASE STUDY**

# Beijing's palace museum embraces renewal

This national museum was established in 1925 after the last Emperor of China was evicted from his palace in the Forbidden City, built around 1420. **The Palace Museum** consists of 980 buildings and covers 72 hectares! The imperial collection of paintings, ceramics and antiquities makes it one of the most prestigious museums in the world. In 1987 it also became a

UNESCO World Heritage site. They have an average of 40,000 visitors a day! There is no doubt that this is one of the most prestigious, award-winning and trusted institutions in the world. But if you have teenagers, you know that all these achievements can mean nothing to them. They often find such things utterly boring and old fashioned, and most youngsters need to be dragged to this type of museum by their parents. How do you hold on to your trusted position while extending it to new target groups? This was the question the Palace Museum asked itself more than a decade ago.

They started by digitizing their vast collection. The extensive use of digital technology allowed them to preserve, present and promote their heritage more easily across a wider selection of target groups. They then optimized visitor services by building an accessible network of useful information. Virtual reality devices, interactive video walls on which pieces of the collection were projected and touch screens with reproductions in 3D helped bring the imperial collection alive virtually. Most of these digital museum experiences could also be downloaded onto the visitors' mobile devices. To digitize the museum

experience, they partnered with telecom operator Tencent. Together with another partner, Huawei, they created a virtual reality mapping experience that provides users with additional educational information.

But they didn't stop there. Going far beyond the usual didactic offering, they also launched a clothing line and cosmetic products based on famous artifacts from the museum's collection, sold online as well as in the museum shops. It took the museum eleven years of work to document and digitize its collection in 3D. They also continued their efforts to open up their museum to the rest of the world by partnering with Google Arts and Culture,[64] where they showcase their top 100 masterpieces. Today they are listed by the American magazine *Fast Company* as one of the top ten most innovative Chinese companies.[65]

With the closure of the museum due to Covid-19, interaction through all these different channels, devices, games, educational tools and products helps make them a reliable partner in the daily lives of many. Today, a new generation in China and abroad will grow up with a trustworthy imperial (digital) experience!

## 3. YOUR COMMUNITIES

After winning the trust of your target group, the next step is to create reliability within the community where you operate. The glowing halo around your company will convince other businesses to join you in that business park, make local governments happy to attract you to their town, and stimulate citizens to want you in their area. Don't underestimate the latter: Amazon pulled out of its plan to build their headquarters in Queens[66] following community backlash, proof of the rising power of citizens.

As explained in earlier chapters, communities comprise a broad range of all possible encounters between your company and the outside world, and your company's relationship to them can be an important metric in evaluating its reputation. The Reputation Institute,[67] for example, releases an annual RepTrak®100 survey that measures corporate reputation, a great tool for global brands to see where they stand on items such as citizenship, financial performance, governance, innovation, leadership, products and services, and workplace satisfaction. In 2020, **Lego**[68] displaced **Rolex** to take the number one position as the most highly regarded company in the world when it comes to corporate reputation. Not bad for a simple toy brand founded in 1932! According to the Reputation Institute's CEO, Kylie Wright-Ford, Lego was rated the most reputable company worldwide because 'Reputation is a balancing act of doing and saying the right thing, and The LEGO Group is a shining example of how to do this purposefully and consistently. An iconic brand that nourishes its heritage, LEGO also innovates with a proven commitment to communities via educational programs and sustainability through the reinvention of their products.'[69]

The company I'd like to highlight now may not dominate the RepTrak 100, but it is nevertheless an inspiring example of how a trustworthy reputation can reap major benefits. A company you may or may not have heard of, operating in the e-commerce fashion industry.

# Portuguese persistence backed by virtue

Farfetch.com[70] is an integrated online marketplace supporting and promoting the retail activities of independent boutiques in the e-commerce sector. I have chosen this company not out of love for fashion, but for the amazing story of its founder, José Neves, which features in Astrid Wendlandt's book[71] *How Luxury Conquered the World.* José is a self-educated Portuguese computer geek who became a retail mogul. The story of Farfetch is special for several reasons. It transformed the industry's e-commerce space by providing a full-service platform to consumers, enabling them to buy from both boutiques and brands directly, and this on a global level.

According to Astrid, who had the opportunity to interview the founder, this is related to José's desire to stay one step ahead of the competition, always. He is constantly thinking about how he can remain relevant, using technology to his advantage. He wasn't always this successful, but when he created Farfetch in 2008, he knew he wanted to become the Amazon of fashion. His patience, openness and trustworthiness created a revolution in the fashion industry. He managed to convince fashion brands and boutiques to collaborate on a level never before seen in this industry. His approach was simple: offering more brands would attract more customers. If the pie grew bigger, there was more for everyone to share.

By 2019 he had partnered with more than 1,000 stores and over 3,000 brands. The platform has over 1.8 million active users and operates in countries such as Brazil, Russia and China in addition to Europe and the United States. José accomplished this by getting rival brands, designers and boutiques to collaborate. Of course, margins and prices were one of the most sensitive issues. Once a garment is sold to a boutique, the online margins are not the same. Many brands also lack the power to set a fixed price list, so prices of the same garment can vary by country and region.

How did he pull this off in an industry known to be full of big, suspicious egos? He proved to the whole fashion community that he was a trustworthy and reliable partner. His platform also rests on certain smart moves he made in the beginning. First and foremost, he was clever enough not to own any stock. This made his company less vulnerable, as owning stock costs a lot of money. Secondly, he negotiated a stunning average of 31% commission on each transaction—most platforms in the e-commerce industry can only dream of such figures!

But there is more than money-making to becoming a reliable partner. He understood that creating a business also meant working on a strong corporate culture. He developed six core values:

• be revolutionary,
• be brilliant,
• be human,
• think global,
• amaze customers, and …
• *todos juntos* (Portuguese for 'all together').

His internal motivational talks are not about becoming the number one fashion platform, but about fuelling enthusiasm. His chief technology officer explains that the company gives each team their own mission. They can come up with their own goals and objectives, a great way to motivate the hundreds of engineers they employ. Many of the staff have worked with José in previous business ventures. They have known each other

for decades. José still keeps them on their toes, but he gives them a second chance if they make a mistake.

Always thinking ahead is what typifies José Neves. As he is in the race with companies like Amazon in the field of online retail technology, he is always thinking ahead. His 'Store of the Future' is just one example of his dream of building an eco-system in which start-ups can connect to the digital world. He believes the future of luxury fashion retail will be defined by the reinvention of the consumer experience, through online and offline integrations. He calls this vision 'Augmented Retail,' taking the magic of the physical store experience and bringing it together with the advantages of the online and digital experience.

Other points of differentiation such as the service 'Second Life', offers pre-loved items to its clients. The concerns of the environmental impact of fashion loom large among a certain age group, and services selling carefully curated second-hand items combined with a Fashion Footprint tool enable fashionistas to continue indulging in their love for fashion, but in an eco-friendlier way. Additional sustainability efforts are made by minimizing the impact of carbon emissions through a variety of measures, including packaging efficiency, renewable energy and carbon offsetting.

With many retail and fashion brands suffering, Farfetch continues to demonstrate the strength of their platform model with continued market share gains. In the first quarter of 2020, revenue increased 90% year-over-year to $331 million. An impressive story from a brand that was built upon the fundaments of trust, the humble character of its founder and the insatiable hunger to do better.

## 4. THE WORLD

There are many ways to build trust and become a reliable brand. Most brands today partner with NGOs or charity projects. This is indeed an effective way to make sure that a part of your revenue or saved earnings goes to dedicated projects in regions or involving issues that count. It is definitely a good first step in showing you care for something or somebody. However, this feels like an add-on to your business concept, and  you will probably end up facing—if you haven't already—a competitor who injects the taking-care-of-the-world part directly into his proposition.

Newly-founded companies make smart use of technology: they not only talk about changing the world, but also act on this desire; they build their entire company around a sustainable, innovative product or service. They might have to build trust in different ways, as they are often solely online players with offices far away—but believe me when I say that Gen Z and younger target groups don't see why that should make any difference when it comes to loving and embracing these brands. Many of these new brands make fascinating cases, and I have picked one in the field of sports and leisure from the land of the kiwi.

# How woolly sneakers are leading the climate-positive race

Have you heard of **Allbirds**? It is a New Zealand-American footwear company founded by Tim Brown and Joey Zwillinger in 2014. They launched their sneakers using a direct-to-consumer approach and are focusing on environmentally friendly footwear. Now, you're probably thinking you've heard this one before, and that this is just one of the many new brands that aim to be eco-friendly. Well, think again: Allbirds is different, which may be one reason why they were valued at $1.4 billion[72] after only two years!

How can such a young company take the lead in the environmental race and become a reliable partner to established major brands such as Adidas? Founder Tim Brown was a professional soccer player in Australia until he retired from the game in 2012. Throughout his career, he was astonished at the cheap materials of his soccer footwear. He wondered why nobody used merino wool—a luxury fabric from Australia and New Zealand—instead of cheap synthetics. In 2014, he brought his ideas to a Kickstarter campaign. It took them two years in research and development to launch their first model in merino wool.

The brand was an instant hit and quickly gained a reputation for quality. Online reviews praised both the comfort of the shoe and the commitment of the brand to environmental sustainability. Allbirds doesn't consider themselves just a shoe company—they want to be a material company. They created other unusual materials like eucalyptus tree fibre and launched another R&D program to develop a carbon-negative sugarcane foam called 'SweetFoam'. This foam is not just any foam: it actually sucks carbon from the air. It took two years to develop and cost millions of dollars to create. Still, they never planned to keep it a trade secret. They published the recipe for SweetFoam, making it available to all interested parties. Releasing their formula was equal parts altruistic and pragmatic, Zwillinger says: 'The altruism is that if everyone uses this, it's going to be great for the environment. The pragmatism is that if everyone uses it, the cost is going to go down.'

But Allbirds is about more than unusual materials. They are a carbon-neutral company. They have rigorously assessed their own carbon footprint across the entire operation, from the raw materials used in the shoes to the carbon employees emit on their commute to work—an amazing achievement to have reached in such a short time. Their reputation for effort and reliability, constructed almost overnight, didn't go unnoticed. Adidas[73] teamed up with them and are planning to combine their respective areas of expertise to create a shoe that has a carbon footprint of just 2 kg compared to the average 12.5 kg of other sneakers on the market. 'Adidas's goal is to sustainably manufacture at scale,' says James Carnes, VP of brand strategy at Adidas. 'When it comes to sustainability, we don't see ourselves competing with one another, but competing for the future. If we don't bring change quickly, there won't be a future to speak of,' says Tim Brown, Allbirds's co-founder. They hope to release the Allbirds/Adidas shoe in 2021.

Neil Blumenthal, the Warby Parker co-founder, considers Allbirds's sustainability efforts crucial to the brand's popularity. 'We're living in the age of the internet, where people can find out every bit of information available,' he said to *Inc Magazine*. 'If you're inauthentic, you're easily found out,' he added. In other words, Blumenthal says: 'It's finally cool to care.' A beautiful example of how reliability and trust can be built by a newcomer in an old industry!

**It is time to be open, transparent, honest and authentic. It is time to dare to admit that perfection doesn't exist.**

# Reliability in a nutshell:

Reliability is key for any brand in any sector with any kind of
target group. If you have it already, you need to work hard
to keep on earning it. If you run a young brand, you'd better
inject reliability into the core of anything you do, as sooner or
later people will find out if you're bullshitting them! Building
reliability is about more than just the rational aspects of your
product. What you stand for, how openly and transparently you
communicate, and how you treat your staff are all ingredients of
the trustworthy relationships you build. Besides, communicating
frankly and openly doesn't cost a thing—and it builds trust.
Remember, trust has become a factor people value almost as
highly as product benefits, and people are looking to companies
to be a trusted guide throughout their lives!

## FREE STUFF YOU CAN DO
## TO BECOME MORE RELIABLE

- Be small. It is easier for small companies to win trust, as they are more approachable.

- Offer a good product and avoid overpromising: two essential pillars on which to build trust.

- Don't over-photoshop your products. It may seem unnecessary and even crazy to mention it today, but many food,[74] fashion and media companies love to sell a version of their product that comes nothing close to reality. Stop lying! Take pictures of the real deal or work harder to make your product look better.

- Become more transparent. Dare to say where you stand in any process, whether it's your sustainability efforts, what has been achieved so far, or what you haven't accomplished yet.

- Communicate frankly and transparently: it costs nothing!

- Dare to let go of your picture perfect brand, no brand is perfect!

- Check your Google reviews, Trustpilot rating and other reliability platforms for citizens. React openly to dissatisfied consumers: this can help in building trust.

# CHAPTER 8

# Why Empathy works

The term 'empathy' is fairly recent: it has only been around for about a century. Today it is actively studied by many cognitive and social psychologists and we still have a lot to learn. It was probably Brené Brown[75] who made talking about vulnerability and empathy conventional. A research professor at the University of Houston, she has spent decades studying courage, vulnerability, shame and empathy. Her 2011 TED Talk[76] made her instantly popular! This video has been viewed over 14 million times, but more importantly, has helped to make people more comfortable talking about the subject.

Brown references Theresa Wiseman's four defining attributes of empathy:
- to be able to see the world as others see it,
- to be non-judgmental,
- to understand another person's feelings, and
- to communicate your understanding of
  that person's feelings.

Brown defines empathy as a skill, stressing the importance of actively practicing the ability to give and receive empathy. This is skill that can be learned and practiced by any human being. Since the C A R E Principles were created as a human-centric philosophy, it is only logical that encouraging brands to think about how they can become more empathic is one of its pillars. You may not think that empathy will make a difference to your business today, but it will definitely give you a head start in tomorrow's world.

## TODAY'S HURDLES

Although it seems like a basic ability we all have, consistent research over the last years shows that empathy is in decline among people of all ages around the world.[77] One reason for this could be related to technology: we all spend a fair amount of time with our noses buried in our smartphones. This encourages us to live inside our digital bubble, without much emotional awareness of others. The digital filter bubble that technology has created on our screens shows us a world filled only with articles, pictures, products and services that we like, and that confirm our point of view. The friends and social contacts we meet in the off- and online world are mostly from the same social class. As a result, people are driven further and further apart. The world seems to be splitting into opposite camps: left versus right, conservative versus liberal, black versus white, poor versus rich … pro versus contra. Nuance seems to have left the building, leaving little or no empathy or understanding for others' point of view.

Yet according to the same research, more than 90% of employees, HR professionals and CEOs state that empathy is important. In business, however, empathy is rarely spotted. An empathic boss might be considered weak by most. Despite a great deal of research proving that empathy matters, many managers try to keep empathy away from the work floor. It is often overlooked as a leadership value, perhaps because it's seen as too soft or too nice. People equate empathy with niceness, although it is not the same thing at all!

One reason for this may be linked to the alpha-male business culture that still prevails throughout a number of industries. Big corporations like France Telecom, Uber and even Nike[78] have been accused of misconduct, bullying and sexual harassment. This type of toxic, non-inclusive leadership leaves no room for a value like empathy. It creates a 'winner-takes-all' mentality that produces organizational dysfunction, with employees treating each other ruthlessly in the scramble to get ahead. Company cultures vary, obviously, but an overall masculine attitude (reflected in expressions such as 'man up') leaves no room to show vulnerability or uncertainty. And distrust of others, unfortunately, is not entirely a thing of the past.

Today, 72% of American CEOs agree that empathy can drive business results; however, that same study[79] shows an 'empathy gap', meaning a *lot of leaders are talking the talk, but are failing to walk the walk!* As empathy in the workplace is fairly new, many CEOs say they struggle to consistently exhibit this, and their employees agree. Many business leaders believe their own company is empathetic, but their staff often disagrees. This disconnect shows that empathy is something that needs to be learnt and acted upon, day in, day out.

**When you think about all the big challenges that we face in the world, empathy is probably the quality we need the most.**

**Jacinda Ardern, Prime Minister New Zealand**

Since the discovery and implementation of empathy in business is still relatively new, the empathy economy is booming. Coaches offering empathy workshops—for a hefty price—are coming out of the woodwork. Be aware, too, that some companies may also try to 'empathy-wash' their message in the same way others 'greenwash' their marketing to look more environmentally friendly.

Empathy can be misused for narrow or short-sighted goals, and, at worst, can even be seen as manipulation. The greatest risk of empathy-washing is that empathy is at a risk of being devalued, as it might be abused by too many leaders trying to sugar-coat reality.

## TOMORROW'S IMPACT

In an age when technology drives many processes and artificial intelligence is still in its infancy, the human side of work will matter more than ever. Our relationships with colleagues, clients, suppliers and business partners will play a major role in the success of our organizations.

The reasons for developing your empathic skills are countless. For this last chapter of the C A R E Principles, let's dive into the universe of your people, your clients, your communities and the world and see how empathy can play a key role in building and maintaining a long-lasting relationship with all of them.

## 1. YOUR PEOPLE

Even though it is fairly new, you may have already guessed from previous chapters that embracing empathy and establishing it at the heart of your organization is key to thriving in the future. Showing you care for your staff and going the extra mile for them will distinguish you from your competitors. It will give you access to the best talent on the market and it will give you the ability to hold onto that talent. Empathetic workplaces tend to enjoy stronger collaboration,[80] less stress[81] and greater employee morale.[82] Empathetic organizations create more value. What are some key elements to work on with an eye toward developing greater empathy within your organization and workplace culture?

The benefits of a strong **company culture** are numerous.[83] It drives the identity and values for a start. It attracts and retains better talent, particularly among millennials. It also increases turnover. But despite the fact that some companies work hard on it, in my experience it is very closely related to the CEO and management. You can have the best company culture ever conceived on paper, but it really only comes alive if it fits the personalities, dreams and ambitions of the CEO. It really comes down to him/her leading by example. Having an empathic internal culture is demonstrated, for instance, in an open-door policy that encourages face-to-face communication.

During the lockdown, Miguel Patricio, CEO of Kraft Heinz, led his company of 38,000 employees spread over 40 countries from his home. He made a habit of making a few random calls each day to some of his employees—all kinds of employees, not just his management teams. He simply asked them how they were coping with the stress of homeworking. In addition, he organized live cooking sessions in his kitchen with his family, inviting 3,000 employees to share this traditional moment of togetherness through digital platforms. These initiatives were not planned or discussed upfront with his management team. It was the spontaneous reaction of an empathic leader who understood that his employees needed to see him as a normal guy at home, spending time in the kitchen with his family. No suits and ties and business calls solely to keep tabs on his staff, but authentic leadership—that is what Miguel Patricio showcased in the midst of the pandemic.

Another sign of empathy is leaving room for failure. It is rare to find a company culture in which it is okay to say you made a mistake. In most cases, people are looking for someone to blame. Openly admitting that one is at fault is still seen as a weakness. Apologizing for doing something wrong is rarely accepted. Punishments for mistakes are still the norm in most companies and the CEO is seen as some kind of divine being who follows a spotless path to success. We all know that this is not reality. Today, a boss who publicly apologizes is still rare. When video communication company Zoom faced security issues due to the skyrocketing number of users during the first lockdown, CEO Eric Yuan apologized and announced what the company would do to fix these problems.[84] Its stock fell 11% after his announcement but quickly picked up again and is sky high today.

Modern leadership includes room for doubt and failure, as the issues ahead of us are complex and challenging, and no boss has superpowers, right? Young employees will demand this type of honest and empathic leadership and will look for bosses who are willing to embrace emotion and show a more vulnerable attitude. According to the 2020 Business Solver Empathy Executive Summary,[85] 83% of Gen Z employees would choose an employer with a strong culture of empathy over an employer offering a slightly higher salary, versus 75% of employees on average. This indicates how the role of empathy in business is just beginning to take hold!

How else can you show empathy towards your people? Offering flexible working hours and understanding the hassle of modern life are just a couple of simple things that employers can do to show they care. Executive Vice President of Telenet Ann Caluwaerts told me that the internal culture at Telenet is female friendly. Late-night working sessions with a quick pizza delivery are not done, as the management understands that young mothers need to go home on time and take care of their children. Obviously, this is also true for young fathers.

With homeworking now embraced by almost all companies, management teams should not invest in digital surveillance software to monitor how much time employees are logged in. Focusing on results instead is a more contemporary way to embrace an empathic leadership style. People who excel in empathy are most successful at leading cross-cultural teams and managing global customers. Understanding others' points of view creates bridges across cultures. So a big loud shout out to all management teams: go look for different people and surround yourself with others to have your company resemble today's streets! No town or city today is filled with white males only! As mentioned earlier, inclusion and diversity are key to fostering an empathic and socially oriented company.

Recognizing and acknowledging the anxiety these turbulent times cause your staff is an important element of a contemporary internal culture. Beyond mental health issues, employees might also show up to work with issues around financial pressure or concerns about a sick loved one or their own health. The pandemic has escalated the importance of all of the above, as fear of becoming infected with Covid-19 is widespread and has made many people anxious about returning to the office. Working on prevention, offering flexible working conditions and acknowledging the difficulty of finding work-life balance is a non-stop process of adjustment. An open dialogue around these issues will remain necessary to tackle them within your company.

> **If you take care of our people, they will take care of your business!**
>
> **Bob Chapman, CEO Barry-Wehmiller**

Finally, offering your employees the opportunity for lifelong learning will help them exercise a flexible, adaptive mindset. Let them learn something new and challenging within the organization before boredom hits. If you can, invest in training programmes, education and all kinds of learning paths to shore up your organization. Knowledge and market trends are evolving at such a pace that it is tough for anyone to keep up.

Unfortunately, the disconnect between skills and knowledge already begins at school. What students are taught and what graduates really need often diverge wildly. In some professions or departments, it might be less of a problem, but in many cases young employees need to be trained from scratch, as their theoretical knowledge is already outdated by the time they reach the job market. Today, most young potentials are given training, but lifelong learning should be made available to all staff.

Now, many of you are probably asking: Does empathy have an impact on business results? Yes it does! Simply because empathy fosters collaboration and teamwork, and this leads to better business results. An Empathy Index published in the Harvard Business Review found that the ten most empathetic companies increased in value more than twice as much as those at the bottom of the index.[86] They also generated 50% more earnings, defined by market capitalization, from one year to the next.

This comes as no surprise, as we learn from Business Solver's research that 74% of employees would work longer hours for an empathic company. By driving improved productivity and talent retention, empathy is more important than ever to achieving critical business goals such as greater profits and lower people turnover. Additionally, each year their State of Workplace Empathy study has found that 80% of employees would switch companies for equal pay if the employer were more empathetic. These trends prove there is a clear connection between empathy and strong business performance.

Finally, for empathy to make an impact, it must be thorough and authentic. It must be true and honest, and not made up by a marketing department or a PR firm. It is, as mentioned before, a top-down characteristic. Forget about it if your CEO has zero credibility in this field. Your CEO, his/her character, attitude and communication style both internally and externally, will drive the empathy performance of your company—or not!

## When we care less about our people, our people become careless.

**Simon Sinek, Optimist and author at Simon Sinek Inc.**

If this sounds superficial to you, the case study below proves that injecting empathy can also make your company thrive in a business-to-business context. Read on to discover how a machine-building company made empathy their driver of success!

**CASE STUDY**

# Barry-Wehmiller builds a better world through business[87]

Barry-Wehmiller is a St. Louis-based global supplier of manufacturing technology.[88] They make big manufacturing machines for industrial clients, such as packaging machines for the paper industry or glass bottle cleaning machines for breweries. They have acquired more than 100 industrial companies around the globe, most of which were struggling to survive. CEO Bob Chapman and his team have deployed a culture-based turnaround in each and every one of these companies, independently of where they were based. Independently of how big or small they were. Independently of how big their financial struggles were.

This successful turnaround is based upon a simple idea: *create a workplace culture that truly values and cares for employees, treat them as you would treat your children, and the rest will take care of itself.* They believe and have repeatedly experienced that if you take care of your people, they will take care of your business! This simple mantra has led to an average yearly growth of 18% and close to zero layoffs of the more than 12,000 people that

work for the company, even during the Covid crisis!

Bob Chapman is convinced that we need a human revolution. He states that 'the industrial revolution created the brokenness we're now feeling, as it began around economic greed. The industrial revolution wasn't founded on the principles of human dignity and human thriving. It was never about creating meaning and purpose. It was around economic wealth through mass production.' His message is clear: 'business could be the most powerful force for good in the world if it simply genuinely cared about the people it had the privilege to lead'.

How did he turn things around, and how does he apply their mission? 'We measure success by the way we touch the lives of people,' he says. It all starts with trust. Trust is a critical component in all personal and professional relationships; however, it's a scarce commodity in our modern world. Specifically, distrust of our leaders is a pervasive problem that severely impacts people's professional lives. People simply don't trust their leaders—political or otherwise. Chapman brings in trust as the first value in the cultural turnaround simply by not firing his staff. Secondly, he trains his employees in leadership skills. His Guiding Principles of Leadership might sound a bit superficial to Europeans, but they come down to respect for oneself and others. Employees learn how to actively listen to each other, develop good communication skills and work on positive feedback and the pursuit of common goals through teamwork and collaboration.

As a privately held $3 billion company, Wehmiller accepts a lower ebitda than the industry standard; however, they are doing extremely well, both financially and in terms of their internal culture. They prove that happy staff can really lead to happy profits! For most of his career, Chapman was a traditional businessman; he only arrived at these caring insights about fifteen years ago, which adds a sense of urgency to his philosophy. His advice to other leaders is simple: forget all the management skills you learned in school and in management classes— that is all about learning to manipulate others for your own success.

Now Chapman and his cohorts have created their own university and are teaching their principles to other corporations. Bob also gives speeches around the globe: he was invited to give a TED Talk and to speak at McKinsey, Harvard University and the Kellogg School of Management about how management education should focus on care more than on money, power and position. Bringing care into the equation is what keeps Bob going. In his focus on the individuals within an institution—starting with your own people first—he too shares in the fundamental values advocated in this book. We can only applaud his initiative and help him spread the message of how care will become the next driver of success!

Some have made cynical remarks about Bob's business case. One could argue that he is just another white, middle-aged man who was lucky enough to inherit a business from his father. Only late in his life, after his personal fortune was made, did he start to 'do good'. That may be true, but I prefer somebody who starts caring late to someone who never cared at all. If all CEOs would follow his example, the world's workplaces would look very different!

## 2. YOUR CLIENTS

Empathy really starts internally, but showing you understand your target group and truly demonstrating that you care for them will be a growth factor too. In an age in which understanding your customers and building relationships with them has become key to standing out, empathy should become your priority. People want brands to feel their challenges and understand their emotions. They want brands to show compassion and empathy for their fears and anxieties: fear

of getting ill, fear of losing their jobs, fear of technology, fear of fake news. With the loss in trust in governments and media described earlier in the chapter on reliability, people are turning to companies to help them. Most people believe that brands can be a powerful force for positive change.

People are really looking to brands and are asking them to step up and listen to their concerns. People want brands to talk openly and transparently about what or who they care for. They need to take a stand publicly and show they share people's feelings about what is going wrong in the world. People want brands to express themselves as if they were people and radiate a friendly, comfortable, trustworthy feeling. A feeling that is recognisable and that lets brands establish connections, almost like friendships with people. Companies are asked to protect their employees at all costs, produce safe products, refrain from spreading fake news and communicate transparently about how, who and where they help. But empathy can be about more than just reacting to social injustice—although that's already quite something!

Empathy can also be about expressing compassion. Showing compassion means putting yourself in another's shoes and truly identifying with their situation. Delta Airlines, for instance, handed out pizza for stranded passengers when delays occurred due to bad weather.[89] They showed they understood how dreadful it is to have your flight cancelled—even if it is due to weather conditions, something not within their control.

We have all had horrible experiences with customer service. You really wonder sometimes if brand owners or management teams have ever tried to get something fixed through their own customer service. Probably not! Who hasn't spent hours in calling queues trying to straighten something out? Automated voice menus, being put on hold or—after endless waiting—finally thinking you've got a real person on the line, and then it turns out to be just another voice recording ... The contract workers at call centres receive scenarios on how to handle the frequently asked questions but have no tools nor knowledge nor decision-making power to really make a difference, let alone show empathy. Empathy is a word that is simply not in their guidelines, leaving behind countless frustrated clients. Research proves that the bigger the brand, the worse the customer service![90]

> ## When you think about all the big challenges that we face in the world, empathy is probably the quality we need the most.
>
> **Jacinda Ardern, Prime Minister**
> **New Zealand**

But frustration and feeling unheard by companies are not the only things worrying people today. Sky-high levels of anxiety, depression and other mental health issues play a large role in people's daily lives. One in six Flemish employees have or risk having a burnout. In 2019, 330 million doses of antidepressants were taken in Belgium alone! All data indicates that our collective mental health is rapidly deteriorating. Even sadder is that our youngsters and children are also suffering from mental health issues. More than 15% of young Belgians surveyed admitted to having psychological issues.[91] These heart-breaking statistics are not isolated cases in Belgium. They reflect an unfortunate worldwide phenomenon. Snapchat understood this and speeded up the launch of their 'Here for you' program during the corona crisis, a new service offering mental health support for their users.[92]

The time is right for brands to show they care, not through a marketing campaign or PR statement, but for real! The case below describes a healthcare brand that was built around empathy— strangely enough, something that is often missing in the healthcare industry.

# How to build a thriving company around empathy

Kara Trott is the CEO and founder of **Quantum Health**,[93] a growing American healthcare navigation and care coordination company. She realised that, ironically, the healthcare industry is not consumer-centric. When you have an acute or chronic health issue, it is difficult to think clearly. On top of that, doctors, specialists and practitioners seem to speak a language that is 90% medical and 10% human. Patients are stressed or preoccupied by their situation, and hospital caregivers have little to no time to spend on patients and their loved ones. Showing empathy and putting themselves in the shoes of their patients seem to have become a rare qualities among healthcare professionals.

Starting from this insight, Trott created a brand based on the belief that the best solutions always come from a deeper understanding of the consumer experience. Showing empathy and appreciation for consumers as people— not as objects for just another sale or transaction—was her starting point.

Quantum Health is based on proprietary use of real-time data, along with a team of expert care coordinators who are trained to use empathy when interacting with consumers early in their healthcare journeys. They believe that 'no one should have to navigate the cost and complexity of healthcare alone'. They call themselves 'big-hearted, fast-thinking people on a mission to make healthcare smarter, simpler and more cost-effective.' How do they do it?

First, the staff is trained in empathic skills, and they understand the values of the company. Secondly, trust is a key element in the company. If the management trusts their team, the team will be trusted by others. Furthermore, Trott states[94] that 'in my experience, inside insight has rarely made as much of an impact as an outside perspective. Look for opportunities to ask questions to consumers or to observe their experience to understand how to improve your products or services. If you always ask the hard questions, you can uncover opportunities you never imagined to truly distinguish your company and brand. As an entrepreneur, your focus may ultimately be on the bottom line, but remember, the road to profitability and growth is paved with a keen understanding of the consumer journey and a team that shares your passion for changing lives.'

According to their website, Quantum Health clients reduce costs by 5.7% on average the first year of collaboration, and 9.2% in the third year. Quantum Health works directly for companies by offering them employee health plans. Today, they help more than a million clients and make $63 million in revenue, not bad for an empathic brand!

## 3. YOUR COMMUNITIES

It may not come as a surprise that showing empathy for communities is a rare business practice. Many industries are complicated and rely on multiple layers of suppliers and sub-suppliers. Despite different types of audit tools, despite contracts with subtractors, despite all kinds of monitoring tools for production processes, it is still very difficult to watch over all the minute aspects of every single business transaction. Many sectors suffer from this phenomenon, but the fashion industry may  be one of the least transparent, with sweatshops, child labour, social issues and polluting practices—to name just a few of the challenges this industry faces.

Taking care of suppliers is definitely not high on the priority list of many fashion companies—yet trustworthy suppliers can be a key differentiating point towards your competitors. Chanel, for instance, understood this long before other fashion brands and started buying specialty ateliers. Building their own network of artisans had already cost the brand $169 million in 2019.[95] 'It is crucial to the brand's heritage that we protect leather manufacturers, embroiderers, feather and flower specialists amongst others and preserve the know-how of the fashion's craft,' said Bruno Pavlovsky, Chanel's president of fashion. Not only acquiring these craftsmen but also investing in training and schooling is part of how Chanel takes care of its communities. Though not every brand depends on the artistic skills of its suppliers to the same extent, understanding and showing empathy towards your communities should be on your agenda no matter what form your brand takes.

Progress is being made in the fashion industry—however slowly—and brands are starting to take a stand when it comes to the health of their supply chains. Whether it is an eco-warrior brand such as Patagonia, now taking the lead in the food industry as well with Provisions,[96] or a smaller brand that shows the world how doing business doesn't equal harming the planet, brands are integrating community care into their operations. Read on to find out how one Dutch woman has taken action by creating a platform that aims to empower consumer and producer one garment at a time. Please meet Jeanne De Kroon, UN ambassador and founder of Zazi Vintage.[97]

**CASE STUDY**

## Zazi Vintage, connecting communities through cloth

There are many things to like about Zazi Vintage. I personally love their Indian artisanal designs, but what I like most about this brand is the forthrightness with which they admit that it is difficult to be sustainable in fashion, as the very system in which they operate is unsustainable by definition. What else makes them stand out from the fashion crowd? They have built a brand around women's artisanal communities worldwide. They partner with small women's enterprises in rural areas in India and Afghanistan. They also collaborate with different NGOs, artisanal groups and the UN Ethical Fashion Initiative all around the world. They work closely with all partners to guarantee decent and fair working conditions, living wages and full transparency to raise living standards in their communities over the long term. In this way, the artisans can gain empowerment, lifting themselves, their families and their communities out of poverty and creating new opportunities. Working in this local and limited edition way comes at a high cost. A cost that Zazi Vintage explains in a very transparent breakdown posted on their website for each garment: the amount that goes into labour, materials, transport, tax, etc.

The brand is vintage because they try to reduce their environmental impact by using already existing fabrics and organic materials. However, they realize that, because they work with artisans from marginalized communities in challenging and remote locations, this change is a journey. They work on raising awareness of the importance of environmental protection while promoting responsible actions such as switching to green energy, water treatment and waste reduction. Change takes time, hence their motto:

'We empower the consumer and the producer one garment at a time'. Zazi is not just another eco-fashion brand. Founder Jeanne De Kroon understood that while taking care of the local Asian communities, she also needed to build her own community. She does that by sharing stories from women around the world. Stories about craftsmanship, travels, impact and their community. So when you buy a piece of Zazi Vintage, you actually buy a story!

## 4. THE WORLD

Doing good for the world just because you care has not been on the agenda of many CEOs. Showing empathy beyond your immediate connections, such as your staff, your customers or your suppliers, is really something different. Overall sustainability efforts can of course be included in this chapter, although it is debatable whether companies take action on this matter because of growing consumer protest, or because they genuinely care and because they are truly empathic.

At the end of the day, it might not be so important to understand where the motivation comes from. What matters is that companies large and small stop their storytelling and become story-makers. I mentioned earlier that small, emerging companies enjoy many benefits: they don't have to carry the weight of the past. Still, it is courageous of multinationals to turn the tide and start advocating positive change. The Dutch-English company Unilever has been a forerunner since Paul Polman, their ex-CEO, decided that CEOs should act like activists. He has repeatedly said that 'It's not good enough anymore to do a side activity like CSR—it has to become an integral part of the company's agenda. Businesses that do this are much better off.'[98] After ten years, he left Unilever a more sustainable, more inclusive and more responsible company. His successor Alan Jope continues to realize the company's vision: 'our vision is a new way of doing business—one that delivers growth by serving society and the planet'. A beautiful example of an old industry giant showing that it can turn things around if led by a CEO on a mission. The case I would like to share with you now, however, is one that might be less well-known, even though this multinational has been working on their social and sustainability efforts for quite some time.

**CASE STUDY**

# Danone[99] becomes an 'entreprise à mission'

This French multinational has over 100,000 employees across 150 plants around the world and generated €25 billion in revenue in 2019. They are massive, and mainly competing in the dairy and water category—two product categories that are under pressure. In 2005, they decided to create a healthier future through food.[100] In 2009, 15,000 Danone managers received a bonus for reducing CO2 emissions, demonstrating that they really meant what they said: this was not just a PR stunt or advertising story. In 2017, they revealed a refreshed logo and a new baseline: 'One planet. One health'. This underlines their belief that people's health and the health of the planet are inherently interconnected. It also marked a call to action, urging consumers to join the 'food revolution' and adopt healthier, more sustainable eating and drinking habits. In addition, Danone aligned with the 2030 Sustainable Development Goals of the United Nations, which include delivering stronger sustainable profitable growth, being an inclusive employer and preserving and renewing the planet's resources.

Danone's CEO Emmanuel Faber is a strong believer in stakeholder capitalism. Yet he is aware that the biggest challenge in turning stakeholder capitalism from a public-relations talking point into a true operating system is metrics. 'We know how to measure returns to shareholders. But how do you measure returns to "stakeholders"? And how do you hold companies accountable for delivering, or not delivering, those returns?' he asked in a Next Leadership podcast.[101] It is by no means easy for a multinational that owns brands selling water in plastic bottles to turn the tide.

Nevertheless, positive change continues at Danone. One key move was their partnering with B Corp,[102] a non-profit organization I mentioned earlier. Since 2015 they have managed to have seventeen Danone entities certified. Danone North America even became the world's largest B Corp, a key social and environmental milestone for the firm that shows it has met the 'highest standards of verified social and environmental performance, transparency and accountability.' Faber is even going a step further, as Danone is the first listed company to adopt the French 'entreprise à mission' model that was created by French law in 2019. Among other things, it means that their social, societal and environmental objectives are written into the company's legal foundations. In the podcast, Faber explains how the shareholders and management team were convinced to change sides. The competitive advantage that the company gets from its social and environmental efforts is the primary reason why they all signed on.

Granted, Danone is the first multinational to adopt this level of transparency and accountability. 'Taking care first of all our stakeholders can only lead thereafter to happy shareholders. Stakeholder capitalism is no longer a choice, it is a necessity.' Danone is now accelerating their environmental efforts, as their food business—and hence their very existence—is at stake, as its core dairy and water operations are under increasing pressure from economic shifts and environmental activists.

This strategy is shared with all employees and a selection of twenty-six elected employees report directly to the board, without even Faber—the CEO—knowing what they will share with the board. They do this because the company believes that the engagement of their people will be an important differentiator in the future. The company's mission has been anchored in its constitution, making it independent of the CEO or board of directors. Faber's own bonus encompasses items such as CO2 reduction and employee engagement, enabling him to maintain focus on these matters and push positive change forward.

Reducing sugars and artificial ingredients to help people improve their eating habits, reusing and reducing plastics and other materials, improving transparency, supporting local farming and tackling climate change are all on the agenda. Step by step, the company makes progress and provides concrete examples of how they care for people and the planet. When asked in the podcast what advice he gives other companies that are only just starting to think about taking up their responsibility, Faber answers: 'A company does not exist to make profit, the reason it exists is because it has a social impact. It has a positive reason for people to engage with you. Start looking at your company from outside, hear the sides you don't like to be hearing from, the critical voices, and genuinely listen to that. The case for change can occur there. Secondly listen to your kids. In 2009 we asked a couple of colleagues to talk to their kids and we filmed it. These kids were between five and fifteen years old. That film in which these kids spoke about the planet, the people, the role of Danone, the good and the bad the company did, was sent to 200 managers worldwide. It changed their perspective! You need to reconnect yourself as a human being, a dad and not a corporate guy in a suit. We don't have time anymore to make profit first and then do good. None of your young employees will stay if you are that kind of leader for long. The competitive advantage is also the case for employee engagement and retention, young people are queuing to work for Danone. Faber's parting shot: 'take risks and start moving and gradually it will work'. Wow—Emmanuel Faber, what an amazing leader, and what an amazing company Danone has become and in only a decade!

I hope this last brand case will inspire both small, emerging brands and multinationals to introduce and apply the C A R E Principles. It may not always be easy, but as Danone and others have shown, it's also not impossible. In fact it's quite simple— it's just a matter of finding the courage to think about the long term, about those around you, and about your moral duty to leave behind something that matters.

People are driven further and further apart by the digital filter bubble that technology has created on our screens, showing us a world filled only with articles, pictures, products and services that we like, and that confirm our point of view.

## Empathy in a nutshell:

There is no quick fix to inject empathy into your company. You can learn through coaching, workshops, books or from a trusted role model, but it is like a muscle that needs to be trained constantly in order to perform at its best. What can help you bring more empathy to the way you do business? Being open to change, embracing that adaptive mindset and showing resilience are all signs of empathy. Understand, too, that empathy needs to be built over time. It is part of an ongoing structural change to your business model and organizational structure. Acknowledge that it is a process that will work tremendously well in some fields and keep on failing in others.

# FREE STUFF YOU CAN DO
# TO BECOME MORE EMPATHETIC

- Take time to listen to the concerns of your staff. Just lending an ear can sometimes be enough to help them in dealing better with the issues they face.

- Understand that, with telework and homeworking becoming the norm, most people's work-life balance has shifted. Avoid full days of digital meetings and leave room for people to have multiple breaks during the day to combat 'Zoom fatigue'.

- Give a compliment instead of pinpointing what went wrong. It takes the same amount of energy but will give you more energy in return. Positive feedback costs nothing and will let the receiver shine!

- Communicate in person. With an overload of internal tools and instant messaging, nothing beats face-to-face communication. Grab a coffee with one of your employees, go for a walk with another, buy them a sandwich and improvise a quick lunch together. Rewards and recognition in small gestures also fuel empathy.

- Establish a library hour: a silent moment can create rest and focus, something everybody can benefit from.

- Schedule shorter meetings with clear agenda points. It can make you more productive! People spend too much time in too many meetings, leaving too little time to really work.

- Whenever possible, organize 'walking meetings'. Steve Jobs from Apple was known for this. Go on a hike if your office is close to nature, or go for a walk in town. It will give you some good exercise. A maximum thirty-minute walk in the open air also stimulates your vitamin D production, so what are you waiting for?

- Don't impose a culture in which late work or taking work home is the norm.

- Allow flexible working hours if possible. Some people like to exercise in the middle of the day, others are most productive early in the morning ... Let go of the 9 to 5 mentality to allow your staff more freedom and less stress.

- Take the advice of Emmanuel Faber, CEO of Danone, and talk to your kids. Talk to them, listen to them and even film them—truth comes from the mouths of babes.

# CHAPTER 9

# Embracing the new kids on the block: Generations Z and Alpha

Having introduced the C A R E Principles and given examples of how you can apply them to your people, your clients, your communities and the world, I would like to share a few last thoughts on the future generations that will work for you—the ones who are out there buying, or who will be buying, your services and products (or not!). You can expect to encounter them in your communities sooner or later.

I am not a fan of trying to pinpoint any target group. Frankly, I hate the term 'target group'—as if people have a bullseye on their back just waiting to be targeted by obnoxious companies that only want their money. In addition, it's no longer considered proper to look at people in a blunt, sociodemographic way, as the process of targeting an audience has become far more diverse and stratified. I refuse to work with 'personas', a tactic still used by many companies, which make customers look like picture-perfect people—*Hello*, who's perfect?

Trying to understand and reach your audiences through tribes, passionate communities or common circles is more inclusive, but still leaves room for exceptions. So, don't see this chapter as a defined profile of upcoming generations, it would completely defeat the purpose of looking at people as people. The reason why this generational overview is included in this book is because I have met many managers who struggle to understand millennials, let alone have a clue about the generations that will follow them into adulthood. There is already sufficient information on millennials, so I'll stick to Generation Z, a digital-native generation born after 1995, and Generation Alpha, born after 2010 and still children. While I agree that labelling things doesn't always help to fully grasp the people involved, it does make it easier for the sake of the discussion to give them a name. In case you are interested in understanding why social researchers identify the groups of generations with X, Y, Z or Alpha, Australian social research bureau McCrindle does a good job of explaining. [103]

Let's dive into **Gen Z** first, as they are coming of age and you'll be meeting them soon professionally. One thing that unites this generation no matter where they live is that they entered into adulthood during a global pandemic. They have known a pre-Covid-19 world and now they have to deal—as the first young generation—with the world created by the disease. Although corona is having a multitude of effects on them, it is clear that this generation suffers more than others from mental health issues.[104] This generation was already dealing with stress, anxiety and depression before the global health crisis, but corona intensified these feelings. Furthermore, they are the most socially-driven generation so far. It is no surprise that Greta Thunberg was Time Person of the Year in 2019![105]

Generation Z is rocking the world with their activism around gun control, climate change, racism, immigration reform, sexism and many other causes. Whether you are a Thunberg fan or not, there is no denying that she and her peers are a force to be reckoned with. They are not only talking about changing the world. They are doing it and are fearless when it comes to holding people in power accountable, no matter how 'powerful' or 'famous' they are. They rely on social media and technology for pretty much everything in their lives. Their phone is their gateway to all forms of communication. Their 24/7 connectivity makes them the most educated generation the world has ever seen. They search until they find access to any type of information they want to find. They'll dig deep into your manicured brand stories and will not be afraid to call you out if you are lying or greenwashing or sugar-coating your stories.

> We are in the beginning of a mass extinction and all you can talk about is money and fairy tales of eternal economic growth, how dare you!
>
> **Greta Thunberg**

They use social media to create movements and to spread their thoughts. They are a generation pursuing purpose and following up on whatever genuinely ignites their passion. However, they are certainly no saints. They might fight passionately for a cause one day and show conflicting behaviour the next. This is quite normal, as they are young, capricious and still finding their way in life. They want to be seen as environmentally conscious but often don't want to pay for it, and they blame adults for the mess the world is in today. In surveys they will say that they prefer environmentally friendly products, organic foods and ethical fashion— but not necessarily if they have to pay for it themselves. They are very aware of money and do not find anything conflicting about buying themselves the cheapest product on the market with their own pocket money, while throwing an ecological tantrum if their parents don't buy the more expensive organic version of it. They don't see anything conflicting in this attitude—to them it is just a matter of smart optimization. They love 'deals' and will research how they can find your product at the lowest price! However, they are prepared to stand up for what they believe in and have no shame in calling out anybody else who is—in their eyes—behaving wrongly in social matters.

They still love brands, especially those that speak out loudly on social matters. In their brand selection, they are easily swayed by video content. They trust their peers more than brands and heavily rely on them for what channel/brand/ platform to follow. They carefully curate their online image, often through 'public' and 'private' accounts. Don't think they are 'naive digital hippies', however: they are very aware of the downsides of their constant connection and of the dangers they may encounter in their online lives. They understand the 'rules' of giving you their data in return for free goodies, but don't blame them if they give you fake phone numbers or fake email addresses. You can easily seduce them into sharing your brand challenge or win action on their own pages, but don't be upset when they unfollow you the day after the win action is over. They understood long before us that their 'lives' had become a transactional good.

**We live in a society now that likes care wherever they are, whether it's medical care, whether it's a delivery service, whether it's ordering movies on Netflix.**

**Samir Qamar, founder and CEO of Medwand**

From companies they expect a wide range of services and features, such as personalization, customization, exclusive or limited products and brand collaborations. They want to be entertained and love loads of different content on branded platforms. However, they live in an interconnected world and are thus accustomed to a flawless customer experience with foreign brands. They watch, like, learn, buy and dream globally, so they won't really be bothered by #buylocal initiatives unless your local brand has gotten their attention for some other reason than being local.

As mentioned before, they are not impressed by whatever glorious past your brand may have had—in fact, if the brand does not bring relevance into their lives, they'll simply ignore it. A remarkable example of this turned up in *De Tijd*,[106] the Flemish business newspaper that interviewed Frederik Delaplace, the new CEO of VRT, a famous Belgian media brand with several TV and radio channels. When Delaplace's appointment as CEO was announced, he had a full day of interviews in TV journals and many congratulatory messages from politicians and powerful businesspeople. When he came home that night, his stepson asked him 'What is that company you started to work for again?' Delaplace admitted laughingly that this remark brought him straight down to earth. A typical remark from Gen Z!

Above all, they like brands that act in a true, honest and authentic way. They hate fake and will burn down their own 'heroes' as quickly as they build them up. Ask TikTok rising star Emmuhlu,[107] who got embroiled in a controversy and quickly lost many of her followers. Or Instagram model Nikita Dragun,[108] who was accused of abusing Photoshop and Facetune software to make herself look thinner and more beautiful. She realized that she was creating a toxic narrative about beauty by showing a version of herself far from reality and finally posted a picture of herself with no makeup and no digital editing. Whatever they dig, this generation has learned to accept the flaws of their online lives faster than most brands, and they are not afraid to embrace failure.

How can you prepare your company to employ them? Despite being a digital generation, they love to have real human contact at work. Collaboration is key to them, and they like building multiple-generation teams, as they are eager to learn from others. Even more than millennials,[109] they strive for a balanced life-work situation. As noted previously, they are open about their mental health issues and are looking for an employer who handles this aspect of their lives with care and consideration. As I have also suggested in previous chapters, the one-time annual job review and personal evaluation won't work for them. They like multiple feedback moments, so you will need to find a regular system of checking in on them, both in real life and digitally. As they are so used to finding out whatever needs to be found out, it is good to integrate them into a horizontal team. They can come up with solutions and angles for problems your more senior people will struggle with. So forget the old school option of putting the junior profile at the bottom of the pyramid. Finally, they mainly see failure as a growth opportunity, so pull them in to change your organization and make it a more agile, fast-forwarding, innovation-driven, caring company. I promise, you won't regret it!

And now a few thoughts on Generation Alpha, most of whom are around eleven years old now, still children on the verge of becoming teenagers. Although they have been the subject of less research, they are the first generation to be fully born in the 21st century, and many if not all of them will live through the 22nd, as they will live longer and enjoy better health. Who knows, they might not even die—the search for eternal youth and the possibility of living on other planets have already been launched by billionaires such as Jeff Bezos and Elon Musk! While the traits that come to define a generation often don't start to manifest until their members reach adolescence or early adulthood, it's possible to identify certain features of Generation Alpha already.

**I need to recognize where consumers want us in ten years ... I believe businesses that are only targeting profits will die.**

Alex Ricard, CEO of Pernod Ricard

The first observation we can make is that this generation is most likely to live in a domestic arrangement that does not include both biological parents. Stepparents, single moms with sperm donors, elderly mums, third-party reproduction methods and LGBTQ[110] parenthood ... these are their children. The traditional mother-father-child family will be only one of many possibilities.

On a global level there will be a higher proportion of children with foreign-born parents and children who are foreign-born themselves, representing more countries around the world than previous generations. McCrindle says: 'This is a generation that move more frequently, will change careers more often and increasingly live in urban, not just suburban, environments.' No wonder racial diversity will become the norm—in addition to greater mobility between countries, demographic shifts indicate that white people may become a minority in many countries where they were once a majority. Gen Alpha will probably also experience economic inequality, an unfortunate observation that can already be seen nowadays with the erosion of the middle class, a phenomenon that started more than a decade ago. A recent study from the OECD shows that many OECD countries[111] —such as the US, Germany, and Belgium—have seen their standard of living stagnate or decline, while higher income groups have continued to accumulate income and wealth.[112]

> **Leave behind more than you take away is our duty on this planet.**
>
> **Ursula Burns, Executive Chairman VEON**

They are definitely the technology generation, as they were born in the year the iPad was released, and Instagram was launched. Ongoing research into the effects technology and always being 'on' have on the brain has produced variable results; however, it is probably safe to say that this generation will enjoy increased digital literacy and love gamified learning but will also have shorter attention spans. Generation Alpha has a very intuitive relationship with screens. Have you ever witnessed the ease with which babies swipe right? They are often called 'screenagers', as the glass they interact with is still 'a wearable device' on their wrist or in their hand. Soon, however, it may be integrated into their bodies. Whereas we might oppose the idea of having a chip or other device implanted in our bodies, they will see it as an extension of their own consciousness and identity. The virtual world will thus collide with the physical, and certain boundaries will become blurred. They may also be the most diverse generation yet, leading some to call them 'the divergents', as they will vary greatly in terms of ethnicity, nativity, income, family situation, etc.

You might also be interested to know that they will be born from now until 2024. Who's next? McCrindle calls the generation born between 2025 and 2039 Generation Beta and predicts that Generations Gamma and Delta will follow. Time will tell if the world will continue to follow this way of labelling generations—or perhaps by that time we will be ready to look at newborns with fresh eyes!

Whatever they dig, Generation Z has learned to accept the flaws of their online lives faster than most brands, and they are not afraid to embrace failure.

# CHAPTER 10

# The C A R E SCAN: How much does your company C A R E?

As I have emphasized throughout this book, applying the C A R E Principles is easy: any brand, big or small, start-up or multinational, can do it. In order to see clearly the areas in which you already excel and which fields could use some more care, I have developed an easy-to-use online tool that you can find on the website Thecareprinciples.com.

A survey will ask questions about all the shifts in attitude explored in this book and will be directed at the four fields in which you can apply the C A R E Principles: your people, your clients, your communities and the world. After filling in this questionnaire, you'll immediately get a diagnosis of where you stand. The C A R E Scan is an indication of what goes well and what you might be able to do better. It is a tool to help you guide your company into a successful future—but as mentioned before, this process doesn't have to be carried out all at once: it can be done step by step. The C A R E Scan is a proprietary methodology developed in collaboration with Ivox.[113] to give you direct insight into where you can best focus in order to prepare your company for the future.

So check it out and take the C A R E Scan now: find out where your company stands on Thecareprinciples.com.

# Thanks!

Where do I start? There are so many people I need to thank for helping me realize this C A R E model and book. I apologize up front for those who I might have forgotten! First and foremost, I would like to thank Rob, my partner, as he always stood by me in the whole process of thinking, researching and writing. He always stepped in and was prepared to listen to my racing thoughts! I also owe a debt of gratitude to my daughters Lua and Rocky, who had to listen to my struggles at many a dinner.

Alexandre Pijcke, a former boss and now business partner, was always there to help me formulate my thoughts and was a huge help in developing the C A R E Scan. Long-time friends such as Hilde, Ingrid, Véronique, Kathy, Godelieve, Els and Charlotte supported from the sidelines in this challenging and transformational year. Several walks with Katia Strauwen and Hanan Challouki have helped me tons in sharpening my ideas and in continuing to invest in this personal transformation of becoming a more caring version of myself. Special mention goes to Alexis Verschueren, who proposed spontaneously and without knowing the content of my book, to help me promote it, free of charge, in a very challenging year for his event business. Wow, Alexis, this gesture touched me profoundly! Thumbs-up to designer Samira El-Kaddouri, who has made the logo and part of the visual identity. Infinite gratitude goes to the very talented illustrator and graphic designer Lucia Biancalana. She created a complete visual world for the C A R E Principles. She understood my vision immediately and, from the very first stroke of the pen, realized a powerful, inclusive world that has shaped the complete vision from book to website. She also collaborated closely with Timo from Dev+, a truely very caring, empathic and great web developer! Copy editor Irene Schaudies turned my basic English text into poetry; I could not have done this without her! And fashion photographer Oona Smet made me look like a rockstar in the pictures that were made to promote this project.

Finally, I would like to thank Niels Janssens from LannooCampus, who believed in my vision from the first draft. He gently pushed this manuscript to become a better version of itself, and, together with the whole team at LannooCampus, I am happy with the result.

2020 has been a hell of a year for most of us, but I must confess that I am happy with my personal transition, as it has made me find my own purpose. I know now that it was time for me, too, to focus on what matters and not on what sells.

# About

Isabel Verstraete started her career in advertising and marketing and worked in France, the Netherlands and her home country, Belgium. She has worked on the corporate side of the fence as well as on the agency side.

Her biggest driver has always been her ability to help brands.

In 2011, she founded her own strategy consultancy and developed the i-scan: a repositioning methodology, applied successfully by dozens of companies from SMEs to multinationals. She has been leading strategic assignments in marketing, branding, strategy, communication and innovation.

Since 2019, she has served as president of FAM: the Female Association of Marketing, a hub of the Belgian Association of Marketing.

In the midst of the pandemic, she started working on the C A R E Principles to provide companies with a new vision and methodology to help them become future-proof by injecting care into everything they do.

Thecareprinciples.com is a platform for positive change. This platform aims to be a clearinghouse for positive ideas that foster these principles, where likeminded brands and business can trade tips, seek out new collaborative ventures, learn new techniques for caring in their own organization, or just get inspired by successful examples—and in this way join hands, however virtually, to build up a network for positive, profitable change.

A great deal of the content you will find here is freely accessible—after all, caring is sharing! But if you want to go deeper, explore further and make contact with experienced players in the field of caring business models, sign up to the C A R E Classes.

Do you have an inspiring example or a compelling idea to share?
Then by all means get in touch! Submit your stories, pictures or proposals to hello@thecareprinciples.com.

# Praise for
# *Does Your Brand Care?*

Business as usual is over. Turbulence will be the new normal. We really need to think about how we live and what we do. This also implies a shift in attitude towards how we do business. This book conveys a new methodology for helping brands to prepare for these extraordinary times. More than ever, we need to focus on what matters, not on what sells.

Caroline Pauwels, Rector Vrije Universiteit Brussel

At Special Olympics Belgium, empathy, trust and respect are the key ingredients in fostering an environment where our athletes can grow and thrive–but also for knitting together the community of volunteers, sponsors and partners that make our work possible. As the C A R E Principles show, these building blocks can be used by anyone in any sector to lay the foundations for a meaningful and sustainable society.

Zehra Sayin, CEO Special Olympics Belgium

Your brand will be stronger, when you genuinely care about your employees. The relations with your customers will be deeper, when you are an empathic employer. Your organization will be more agile, when your teams are truly empowered. The C A R E principles described in this book bridge the gap between People and Marketing. They are the two sides of your company's identity. I am convinced this book will spark great conversations between Marketing and HR, making your company and brand more authentic, agile and simply better.

Ann Caluwaerts, Executive Vice President Telenet

# End notes

[1] https://plusmagazine.knack.be/recht-en-geld/belg-neemt-gemiddeld-34-dagen-per-jaar-vrij/article-news-1569579.html

[2] I prefer the 'next normal' compared to the 'new normal', as we will be facing many 'new normals' in the years ahead.

[3] https://bcorporation.net/

[4] https://www.edelman.com

[5] https://www.edelman.com/trustbarometer

[6] https://www.edelman.com/sites/g/files/aatuss191/files/2019-06/2019_edelman_trust_barometer_special_report_in_brands_we_trust.pdf

[7] https://news.bloomberglaw.com/daily-labor-report/obama-backed-netflix-documentary-causes-headaches-for-fuyao-glass

[8] https://www.theguardian.com/environment/2014/oct/04/wwf-international-selling-its-soul-corporations

[9] https://www.loom.com/

[10] https://www.thesun.co.uk/tech/11254108/coronavirus-impacted-schools-offered-unlimited-zoom/

[11] https://www.standaard.be/cnt/dmf20190715_04511441

[12] patagonia.com

[13] http://www.patagoniaworks.com/press/2019/9/19/facing-extinction

[14] https://dictionary.cambridge.org/dictionary/english/kpi: key performance indicator: a way of measuring a company's progress towards the goals it is trying to achieve

[15] https://www.youtube.com/watch?v=L4YtgliGfKg

[16] https://www.cleveland.com/entertainment/2020/08/snow-patrols-releases-crowd-sourced-new-recording-the-fireside-sessions-ep.html

[17] https://www.winsightgrocerybusiness.com/retailers/aldi-mcdonalds-make-staff-sharing-deal-germany

[18] https://www.winsightgrocerybusiness.com/retailers/sedanos-local-restaurants-work-together-keep-staff-employed

[19] New product development.

[20] Nondisclosure agreement is a contract through which the parties agree not to disclose information covered by the agreement. An NDA creates a confidential

relationship between the parties, typically to protect any type of confidential and proprietary information or trade secrets.

[21] https://www.diageo.com/en/news-and-media/features/diageo-announces-creation-of-world-s-first-ever-100-plastic-free-paper-based-spirits-bottle/

[22] https://www.pilotliteventures.com/

[23] https://www.pulpex.com/

[24] https://www.bbc.com/future/article/20200420-coronavirus-why-some-racial-groups-are-more-vulnerable

[25] https://www.bbc.com/worklife/article/20200617-the-luxury-and-privilege-of-a-balcony-or-yard-during-covid

[26] https://www.insurancebusinessmag.com/au/news/breaking-news/iag-rolls-out-new-workplace-flexibility-app-173425.aspx

[27] https://www.ft.com/content/bd1b4158-09a7-11ea-bb52-34c8d9dc6d84

[28] https://www.solvay.com/en/

[29] https://www.weforum.org/reports/gender-gap-2020-report-100-years-pay-equality

[30] https://www.businessinsider.nl/why-women-almost-never-become-ceo-2016-9?international=true&r=US

[31] https://www.imdb.com/title/tt6857988/

[32] https://www.cnbc.com/2018/03/02/why-companies-with-female-managers-make-more-money.html

[33] http://www.chinadaily.com.cn/business/2017-07/10/content_30061241.htm

[34] https://www.statista.com/statistics/248769/age-distribution-of-worldwide-instagram-users/

[35] https://retailtrends.nl/news/60595/zeeman-boekt-meer-omzet-met-minder-winkels

[36] https://www.mirror.co/

[37] https://www.onepeloton.com/

[38] https://www.billionavenue.com/

[39] https://www.tijd.be/ondernemen/technologie/barco-ziet-start-upidee-clickshare-uitgroeien-tot-sterkhouder/10118217.html

[40] https://www.youtube.com/watch?v=drcO2V2m7lw

[41] https://www.youtube.com/watch?v=C9I-W1eTCbk

[42] https://www.chipotle.com/

[43] https://www.businessinsider.com/chipotle-hasnt-overcome-e-coli-fears-2018-3?international=true&r=US&IR=T

[44] https://www.businessinsider.nl/chipotle-taco-bells-ceo-changes-2018-2?international=true&r=US

[45] https://www.youtube.com/watch?v=MFmr_TZLpS0

[46] https://www.mobilemarketer.com/news/chipotle-smashes-tiktok-records-with-guacdance-challenge/560102/

[47] Generation Z is the generation born between 1996 and 2010. Generation Alpha is born between 2010 and 2024; more info about these target groups in chapter 8.

[48] http://www.pave-marolles.be/a-lhotel-galia-la-porte-est-ouverte/

[49] This effect grants the power to cause a hurricane in China to a butterfly fluttering its wings in New Mexico. It may take a very long time, but the connection is real. If the butterfly had not fluttered its wings at just the right point in space/time, the hurricane would not have happened.

[50] https://www.energycommunity.org/documents/copenhagen.pdf

[51] https://commercial.cnn.com/why-trust-relevance-reliability-matters-news-consumers

[52] https://www.cleanenergywire.org/factsheets/dieselgate-timeline-car-emissions-fraud-scandal-germany

[53] https://www.statista.com/chart/17467/annual-expenditure-on-climate-lobbying-by-oil-and-gas-companies/#:~:text=The%20world's%20five%20largest%20publicly,blocking%20binding%20climate%2Dmotivated%20policy.

[54] https://www.businessinsider.nl/toblerone-gate-chocolate-bars-shrink-to-cut-costs-2016-11?international=true&r=US

[55] https://www.theguardian.com/commentisfree/2019/oct/23/exxon-climate-change-fossil-fuels-disinformation

[56] https://www.bbc.com/news/world-us-canada-48262567

[57] https://www.cnbc.com/2020/06/18/bankrupt-hertz-terminates-controversial-stock-sale.html

[58] https://www.businessinsider.nl/facebook-twitter-finally-stood-up-trump-2020-6?international=true&r=US

[59] https://www.edelman.be/research/edelman-trust-barometer-2020

[60] https://www.accenture.com/_acnmedia/pdf-109/accenture-ungc-ceo-study.pdf

[61] https://www.globalgoals.org/

[62] https://www.studiebureaujonckheere.be/

[63] https://www.liantis.be/nl/nieuws/liantis-awards-2019-winnaars

[64] https://en.dpm.org.cn/about/news/2017-05-19/2647.html

[65] https://www.fastcompany.com/90457942/china-most-innovative-companies-2020

[66] https://www.nytimes.com/2019/02/14/nyregion/amazon-hq2-queens.html

[67] https://www.reptrak.com

[68] https://www.reptrak.com/global-reptrak-100/

[69] https://www.lego.com/en-us/aboutus/news/2020/march/reptrak/

[70] https://www.farfetch.com/

[71] https://www.misstweed.com/book-HOW-LUXURY-CONQUERED-THE-WORLD.html

[72] https://www.inc.com/cameron-albert-deitch/allbirds-2018-company-of-the-year-nominee.html

[73] https://www.fastcompany.com/90510038/adidas-and-allbirds-join-forces-to-design-the-worlds-most-sustainable-shoe?partner=rss&utm_source=rss&utm_medium=feed&utm_campaign=rss+fastcompany&utm_content=rss?cid=search

[74] https://www.youtube.com/watch?v=6HNucx1MaF0

[75] https://brenebrown.com/

[76] https://www.youtube.com/watch?v=iCvmsMzlF7o

[77] https://www.businessolver.com/

[78] https://hbr.org/2018/11/how-masculinity-contests-undermine-organizations-and-what-to-do-about-it?registration=success

[79] https://www.businessolver.com/

[80] https://www.nytimes.com/2016/02/28/magazine/what-google-learned-from-its-quest-to-build-the-perfect-team.html

[81] https://www.sciencedirect.com/science/article/abs/pii/S074959781000066X

[82] https://www.annualreviews.org/doi/pdf/10.1146/annurev-orgpsych-031413-091221

[83] https://www.forbes.com/sites/larryalton/2017/02/17/why-corporate-culture-is-becoming-even-more-important/#40fb503a69da

[84] https://www.cnbc.com/2020/04/02/zoom-ceo-apologizes-for-security-issues-users-spike-to-200-million.html

[85] https://info.businessolver.com/hubfs/empathy-2018/businessolver-empathy-executive-summary.pdf?hsCtaTracking=7e237aa9-1d60-4cfb-b9a9-2b881143391a%7C0c012412-b9e0-488a-8f56-4c153450c4fa

[50] https://hbr.org/2016/12/the-most-and-least-empathetic-companies-2016

[87] I was almost finished writing this book when I listened to a podcast by Simon Sinek in which he interviews Bob Chapman, CEO of Barry-Wehmiller, a company I had never heard of. While my C A R E Principles are very close in spirit to his leadership model, I decided to go ahead anyway: there can never be enough people who strive for positive change! Check out the podcast here: https://www.youtube.com/watch?v=T_ysqiRw9fc

[88] https://www.barrywehmiller.com/

[89] https://edition.cnn.com/2017/04/06/us/delta-delays-pizza-trnd/index.html

[90] https://hbr.org/2019/02/why-is-customer-service-so-bad-because-its-profitable

[91] https://www.vrt.be/vrtnws/nl/2019/09/23/grootschalig-onderzoek-naar-psychische-klachten-bij-tieners/

[92] https://www.socialmediatoday.com/news/snapchat-launches-new-here-for-you-mental-health-resource-ahead-of-time-i/574507/

[93] https://quantum-health.com/

[94] https://www.fastcompany.com/90462354/how-i-built-a-63-million-company-around-empathy

[95] https://www.vogue.co.uk/news/article/chanel-acquisitions-craft-ateliers

[96] https://www.patagoniaprovisions.com/

[97] https://www.zazi-vintage.com/

⁹⁸  https://www.ns-businesshub.com/business/paul-polman-unilever/

⁹⁹  https://www.danone.com/

¹⁰⁰ https://www.danone.com/impact.html

¹⁰¹ https://podcasts.apple.com/us/podcast/id1501891506

¹⁰² https://www.danone.com/about-danone/sustainable-value-creation/BCorpAmbition.html

¹⁰³ https://mccrindle.com.au/

¹⁰⁴ https://www.businessinsider.com/gen-z-mental-health-coronavirus-george-floyd-protests-2020-6

¹⁰⁵ https://time.com/5746486/person-of-the-year-2019-editors-letter/

¹⁰⁶ https://www.tijd.be/tech-media/media-marketing/het-kan-best-dat-ik-een-compromisfiguur-ben-maar-dat-zal-me-niet-tegenhouden/10252498

¹⁰⁷ https://www.hitc.com/en-gb/2020/04/27/tiktok-fans-react-to-emmuhlus-apologies-after-n-word-video-surfa/

¹⁰⁸ https://www.dexerto.com/entertainment/nikita-dragun-drags-critics-accusing-her-of-using-too-much-facetune-1296842

¹⁰⁹ https://www.forbes.com/sites/ashleystahl/2019/09/10/how-generation-z-will-revolutionize-the-workplace/#45af8b7f4f53

¹¹⁰ LGBTQ is an acronym for lesbian, gay, bisexual, transgender and queer or questioning.

¹¹¹ https://www.oecd.org/about/document/list-oecd-member-countries.htm

¹¹² https://www.oecd.org/els/soc/OECD-middle-class-2019-main-findings.pdf

¹¹³ https://www.ivox.be